At Issue

IForeign Oil Dependence

Other Books in the At Issue Series:

At Issue

I Foreign Oil Dependence

Ronald D. Lankford, Jr., Book Editor

GREENHAVEN PRESS
A part of Gale, Cengage Learning

GALE
CENGAGE Learning·

Detroit • New York • San Francisco • New Haven, Conn • Waterville, Maine • London

GALE
CENGAGE Learning·

Elizabeth Des Chenes, *Director, Publishing Solutions*

© 2013 Greenhaven Press, a part of Gale, Cengage Learning.

Gale and Greenhaven Press are registered trademarks used herein under license.

For more information, contact:
Greenhaven Press
27500 Drake Rd.
Farmington Hills, MI 48331-3535
Or you can visit our Internet site at gale.cengage.com

For product information and technology assistance, contact us at

Gale Customer Support, 1-800-877-4253
For permission to use material from this text or product, submit all requests online at www.cengage.com/permissions

Further permissions questions can be e-mailed to permissionrequest@cengage.com

Articles in Greenhaven Press anthologies are often edited for length to meet page requirements. In addition, original titles of these works are changed to clearly present the main thesis and to explicitly indicate the author's opinion. Every effort is made to ensure that Greenhaven Press accurately reflects the original intent of the authors. Every effort has been made to trace the owners of copyrighted material.

Cover image © Images.com/Corbis.

LIBRARY OF CONGRESS CATALOGING-IN-PUBLICATION DATA

Foreign Oil Dependence / Ronald D. Lankford, Jr., book editor.
 p. cm. -- (At issue)
 Includes bibliographical references and index.
 ISBN 978-0-7377-6177-1 (hardcover) -- ISBN 978-0-7377-6178-8 (pbk.)
 1. Petroleum industry and trade--Government policy--United States. 2. Petroleum industry and trade--Political aspects--United States. 3. Energy policy--United States. 4. Petroleum conservation--United States. I. Lankford, Ronald D., 1962-
 HD9566.F673 2012
 338.2'72820973--dc23

2012012535

Printed in the United States of America
 1 2 3 4 5   16 15 14 13 12

FD234

Contents

Introduction

According to the US Energy Information Administration (EIA), the United States imported nearly half of its oil (49%) in 2010. This fact, however, reveals very little: the US imports high percentages of many products, from coffee to rubber. The fact that the US imports nearly 50% of its oil, then, fails to make clear 1) how much oil the US requires daily, 2) how essential oil is to US energy needs, and 3) how indispensable energy is to the well-being of the US economy. To better understand what oil dependence means, these questions must be answered.

At the beginning of 2012, the US required nearly 19 million barrels of oil per day to meet its energy needs. At 42 gallons per barrel, that equals nearly 800 million gallons of oil per day. If the US requires 19 million barrels per day for its energy needs, then nearly 9.5 million barrels of oil have to be imported each day, equaling almost 3.5 billion barrels of oil per year. With a slowdown in oil imports, everyday life in the US would quickly feel the impact; with severe shortages, everyday life in the US would come to a standstill.

As an essential energy source, oil powers everything from cars, to airplanes, to construction equipment. Oil products keep trains and supply trucks moving, and oil provides heat for homes; oil products make fuel for military vehicles, and oil is used as a lubricant for machinery and combustion engines. Using data from the EIA, *The New Republic* broke down the use of oil by category:

- 47% Passenger Travel

- 18% Freight

- 15% Heat

- 13% Products and Pavement

- 2% Construction Equipment

- 2% On-Farm Use

- 1% Military

- 1% Recreation

- 1% All Other

Sierra magazine offered a similar breakdown, noting the use of barrels of oil per day in different categories:

- 8.9 million Cars and Light Trucks

- 2.36 million Big Trucks and Buses

- 1.37 million Air Travel

- .89 million Heating

- 6.11 million Electricity, Military, Plastic, and Other Uses

Looking at both sets of numbers, it becomes evident how integral oil is to America's everyday energy needs. Farming, for instance, requires oil-based fuel to run machinery that will plant and harvest agricultural products; delivery trucks require fuel to deliver these products to grocery stores; and grocery stores require electricity to stock these goods in a temperature-controlled environment. And while heating oil may seem much less in demand than fuel for transportation, it services eight million buildings in the US.

In addition to providing fuel for everyday transportation, electricity, and heating, oil is essential to the US military. The military reportedly used 360,000 barrels of oil per day in 2009 at a cost of $13.3 billion dollars. "Although this may seem small," noted *The Daily Energy Report*, "the fact is that DoD [Department of Defense] is the largest single consumer of energy in the United States."[1] When US military personnel are

---

1. Sohbet Karbuz, "How Much Energy Does the U.S. Military Consume?" *Daily Energy Report*, January 3, 2011. www.dailyenergyreport.com.

located at outposts around the world, even the cost of delivering fuel—by transport ships, aircraft, and supply trucks—is massive.

Oil imports depend on availability, an issue that has become more relevant over time due to a finite supply of fossil fuels. When an oil source becomes depleted, a new one must be located. Furthermore, as the world's population increases and more countries compete for the same limited supply of oil, prices become less predictable. When this happens, importing oil becomes more difficult and costly, potentially leading to shortages and price spikes. Oil shortages and price spikes, however, can be caused by other reasons, including market instability.

Many economists cited rising oil prices as contributing to the onset of the US recession in 2007 and 2008. Ryan Avent wrote in *American Prospect*, "In fact, the oil spike of 2008 . . . was an integral part of the economic storm that assailed the nation last fall."[2] While gas prices have a direct effect (many Americans may choose to drive less), these prices also have many indirect effects. For instance, with a higher percentage of income tied to fuel costs, Americans will spend less on groceries, eating out at restaurants, and retail shopping. Likewise, the higher cost of fuel increases the costs of transporting goods and services by freight, leading to inflation. Higher gas prices, then, create a ripple effect within the US economy.

While oil price spikes can be caused by a number of factors, oil shortages can potentially lead to more serious economic problems that impact daily life. With severe oil shortages and higher gas prices, many things that Americans take for granted—like driving a car to school or work each day—may become a luxury. As a result, more Americans might be forced to live near workplaces and shopping centers, perhaps leading to more crowded urban areas. Likewise, because oil

---

2. Ryan Avent, "Did Your Car Cause the Crisis?" *American Prospect*, May 20, 2009. http://prospect.org.

has been essential to economic development, severe shortages would impact the growth of businesses and the availability of products. Without a stable fuel supply, even the response time of the US military might slow down.

The future struggle over oil dependency will remain difficult to resolve. Increasing oil production domestically may decrease imports, while not necessarily decreasing the price of oil. Other solutions, such as developing public transportation, have the potential to decrease fuel use but will take years to develop. Technology may allow scientists to explore new oil resources, but the cost of developing these sources may be prohibitive. In the end, it is likely that multiple solutions will be required to meet America's future energy needs.

The US imports many other products besides oil and many countries, like Japan, are even more dependent on foreign oil. The problem, however, remains the sheer quantity of oil that the US uses, and the importance of that oil for America's everyday energy needs. Oil is simply the lifeblood of the US economy, and any shortage of oil signals potential problems for many aspects of American life.

1

Oil Dependence: An Overview

Russell McLendon

Russell McLendon writes for Mother Nature Network.

The United States is highly dependent on imported oil and this is problematic for several reasons. A number of countries from which the United States imports oil are either unstable or unfriendly, creating potential supply problems. A larger problem, perhaps, is that the world's oil supply is finite. While the United States has been able to meet its energy needs by importing from a wide range of countries, eventually many prime oil sources will dry up. As long as the United States imports the majority of its oil, meeting daily demands will be difficult.

Oil helped fuel the United States' prosperous 20th century, and the growing country built its infrastructure with that in mind. But the sprawling suburbs and far-flung freeways ended up locking America into long-term dependence on the nonrenewable sludge, which passed coal as the nation's favorite fossil in 1951.

U.S. oil production peaked 19 years later, and America suddenly was faced with outsourcing a pillar of its business model. From 1900 until 1969, the country's oil imports had risen by an average of 70.7 million barrels per decade, but in the '70s they rose by nearly 1.9 billion. Making matters worse was political instability in the Middle East, where the United States got much of its imported oil at the time. Following the

1973 Yom Kippur War and again during the 1979–'81 Iran hostage crisis, Americans cut back on oil use, and gasoline consumption dipped for the first time since World War II. But that conservative spirit didn't last.

Despite building a friendlier portfolio of oil providers since the '70s ... the United States still heavily relies on several complicated sources.

The United States now imports almost twice the oil it produces—and is also the world's top overall petroleum consumer, going through 19.5 million barrels a day. While about 13 percent of U.S. oil imports still come from the Persian Gulf, nearly half now originate in the Western Hemisphere, mainly Canada, Mexico and Venezuela. Canada has become the United States' top oil source, sending 99 percent of its exports here, about 2 million barrels a day.

Supply and Command

Despite building a friendlier portfolio of oil providers since the '70s, however, the United States still heavily relies on several complicated sources. About 1.6 million barrels a day still come from the Persian Gulf—enough to yield 32 million gallons of gasoline, fueling roughly 2 million cars with 16-gallon gas tanks. And while longtime ally Saudi Arabia supplies most of that (nearly 660 million barrels in 2008), history has shown international oil alliances can fluctuate wildly. Iraq (229 million barrels), Kuwait (80 million) and Oman (6.7 million) are also consistent Middle Eastern sources.

Another 19 percent of U.S. oil imports come from Africa, mainly Nigeria (361 million barrels in '08). That country's pipelines and other oil facilities have suffered from militant attacks since 2005—including vandalism, kidnappings and violent takeovers—causing some foreign workers and companies to flee. Other top African suppliers of U.S. oil include Algeria (200 million barrels), Angola (188 million), Libya (38 million), Chad (38 million) and Equatorial Guinea (28 million).

Western Hemisphere sources present problems, too. Venezuela has had a belligerent political relationship with the United States in recent years; while it exported about 380 million barrels of crude oil here in 2008, that's down from 474 million in 2004 and 508 million in 1997. Mexico, currently the United States' No. 3 overall foreign supplier, is beginning to suffer its own drop in production, and many analysts believe Mexican oil production has already peaked.

A Line in the Sands

Even oil from Canada—close to the United States politically, culturally and geographically—carries baggage. Output has steadily declined in the crude oil fields Canada relied on for the last 50 years, and while the country has had success with oil shale and offshore drilling, neither is as efficient or simple.

Oil shale is to oil much like lignite is to coal: an undercooked, premature version of it.

Oil shale, a sludgy sediment embedded in deposits called tar sands or oil sands makes up nearly half of all Canadian oil output and is expected to grow in coming years, more than offsetting the country's dwindling production of conventional crude. In addition to reaping the benefits of the vast tar sands to the north, the United States also has the largest oil shale deposits in the world—holding up to 1.8 trillion barrels of petroleum—underneath the Rocky Mountains, especially Colorado, Utah and Wyoming.

But getting oil this way is a messy, expensive and energy-intensive process. Oil shale is to oil much like what lignite is to coal: an undercooked, premature version of it. Oil began as ancient aquatic organisms that settled to the bottoms of seas and lakes after they died, became buried in the Earth's crust, and were pressed and heated over hundreds of millions of years. Oil shale is simply oil that's not as far along in this process, having been subjected to less pressure and heat over the millennia.

Since it's solid, bitumen (the heavy oil extracted from the shale) must be mined rather than pumped, which means extracting it often carries all the same ecological dangers of strip mining and open-pit mining. It also requires heavy use of natural gas and water, which further adds to the environmental footprint of using oil as fuel. And once the shale is mined, it must be heated up to extremely high temperatures to extract liquid petroleum from it, a process that has kept oil shale from being commercially viable almost everywhere but Canada.

Even at half of today's consumption rate, U.S. oil reserves would be used up in 60 years.

Low Reservations

Aside from its untapped oil shale deposits, the United States has about 21 billion barrels of proven oil reserves, which includes drillable reservoirs as well as oil-storage facilities like the Strategic Petroleum Reserve—underground salt caverns along the Gulf Coast that contain the world's largest emergency supply of crude oil. American oil usage would certainly drop if imports somehow dried up, but even at half of today's consumption rate, U.S. oil reserves would be used up in 60 years. Worldwide, half of all commercially available oil may have already been depleted; even conservative estimates expect oil production to peak by 2040.

There are still untapped oil deposits scattered around the world—including some on North America's Outer Continental Shelf and other offshore areas—and even deeper pockets of oil shale in the Rocky Mountains. But as the U.S. Geological Survey points out, "The simple inescapable fact is that the world's supply of petroleum is finite and nonrenewable."

But until natural gas and renewable sources begin filling enough of its energy needs, the United States will likely continue pouring oil on troubled waters. And since Americans still use four times more crude every day than the country can produce itself, much of that oil will likely cross troubled waters to get here, too.

2

Foreign Oil Dependence Threatens US Economic and National Security

Rebecca Lefton and Daniel J. Weiss

Rebecca Lefton is a Policy Analyst with the Energy team at American Progress; Daniel J. Weiss is a Senior Fellow and the Director of Climate Strategy at American Progress.

The United States relies heavily on fossil fuels for its energy needs, tying the country's future economic security to oil imports. This is problematic for a variety of reasons. The United States currently imports oil from a number of unstable nations, potentially helping to finance terrorism. Also, American oil consumption contributes to global warming. By creating extremes in climate changes, global warming is responsible for multiple environmental crises. These crises are expensive and often require increasingly scarce military resources. Even as US oil consumption creates a more dangerous world, the oil industry lobbies against change: importing oil is extremely profitable to the oil industry. In the long run, however, clean energy technology has the potential to create more jobs and bolster a sagging US economy.

A recent report on the November 2009 U.S. trade deficit found that rising oil imports widened our deficit, increasing the gap between our imports and exports. This is but one example that our economic recovery and long-term growth is

Rebecca Lefton and Daniel J. Weiss, "Oil Dependence Is a Dangerous Habit," Center for American Progress online, January 13, 2010. www.americanprogress.org. Copyright © 2010 by Center for American Progress. All rights reserved. Reproduced by permission.

inexorably linked to our reliance on foreign oil. The United States is spending approximately $1 billion a day overseas on oil instead of investing the funds at home, where our economy sorely needs it. Burning oil that exacerbates global warming also poses serious threats to our national security and the world's security. For these reasons we need to kick the oil addiction by investing in clean-energy reform to reduce oil demand, while taking steps to curb global warming.

In 2008 the United States imported oil from 10 countries currently on the State Department's Travel Warning List, which lists countries that have "long-term, protracted conditions that make a country dangerous or unstable." These nations include Algeria, Chad, Colombia, the Democratic Republic of the Congo, Iraq, Mauritania, Nigeria, Pakistan, Saudi Arabia, and Syria. Our reliance on oil from these countries could have serious implications for our national security, economy, and environment.

As a major contributor to the global demand for oil the United States is paying to finance and sustain unfriendly regimes.

Oil Imports Fuel "Dangerous or Unstable" Governments

The United States imported 4 million barrels of oil a day—or 1.5 billion barrels total—from "dangerous or unstable" countries in 2008 at a cost of about $150 billion. This estimate excludes Venezuela, which is not on the State Department's "dangerous or unstable" list but has maintained a distinctly anti-American foreign and energy policy. Venezuela is one of the top five oil exporters to the United States, and we imported 435 million barrels of oil from them in 2008.

As a major contributor to the global demand for oil the United States is paying to finance and sustain unfriendly regimes. Our demand drives up oil prices on the global market, which oftentimes benefits oil-producing nations that don't sell to us. The Center for American Progress finds in "Securing America's Future: Enhancing Our National Security by Reducing Oil Dependence and Environmental Damage," that "because of this, anti-Western nations such as Iran—with whom the United States by law cannot trade or buy oil—benefit regardless of who the end buyer of the fuel is."

Further, the regimes and elites that economically benefit from rich energy resources rarely share oil revenues with their people, which worsens economic disparity in the countries and at times creates resource-driven tension and crises. The State Department cites oil-related violence in particular as a danger in Nigeria, where more than 54 national oil workers or businesspeople have been kidnapped at oil-related facilities and other infrastructure since January 2008. Attacks by insurgents on the U.S. military and civilians continue to be a danger in Iraq.

America's voracious oil appetite continues to contribute to another growing national security concern: climate change.

Our oil dependence will also be increasingly harder and more dangerous to satisfy. In 2008 the United States consumed 23 percent of the world's petroleum, 57 percent of which was imported. Yet the United States holds less than 2 percent of the world's oil reserves. Roughly 40 percent of our imports came from Canada, Mexico, and Saudi Arabia, but we can't continue relying on these allies. The majority of Canada's oil lies in tar sands, a very dirty fuel, and Mexico's main oil fields are projected to dry up within a decade. Without reducing our dependence on oil we'll be forced to increasingly look to more antagonistic and volatile countries that pose direct threats to our national security.

Climate Change Is a Major Threat

Meanwhile, America's voracious oil appetite continues to contribute to another growing national security concern: climate change. Burning oil is one of the largest sources of greenhouse gas emissions and therefore a major driver of climate change, which if left unchecked could have very serious security global implications. Burning oil imported from "dangerous or unstable" countries alone released 640.7 million metric tons of carbon dioxide into the atmosphere, which is the same as keeping more than 122.5 million passenger vehicles on the road.

Recent studies found that the gravest consequences of climate change could threaten to destabilize governments, intensify terrorist actions, and displace hundreds of millions of people due to increasingly frequent and severe natural disasters, higher incidences of diseases such as malaria, rising sea levels, and food and water shortages.

A 2007 analysis by the Center for American Progress concludes that the geopolitical implications of climate change could include wide-spanning social, political, and environmental consequences such as "destabilizing levels of internal migration" in developing countries and more immigration into the United States. The U.S. military will face increasing pressure to deal with these crises, which will further put our military at risk and require already strapped resources to be sent abroad.

Global warming-induced natural disasters will create emergencies that demand military aid, such as Hurricane Katrina at home and the 2004 Indian Ocean tsunami abroad. The world's poor will be put in the most risk, as richer countries are more able to adapt to climate change. Developed countries will be responsible for aid efforts as well as responding to crises from climate-induced mass migration.

Global Warming and the Military

Military and intelligence experts alike recognize that global warming poses serious environmental, social, political, and military risks that we must address in the interest of our own defense. The Pentagon is including climate change as a security threat in its 2010 Quadrennial Defense Review, a congressionally mandated report that updates Pentagon priorities every four years. The State Department will also incorporate climate change as a national security threat in its Quadrennial Diplomacy and Development Review. And in September the CIA created the Center on Climate Change and National Security to provide guidance to policymakers surrounding the national security impact of global warming.

Leading Iraq and Afghanistan military veterans also advocate climate and clean-energy policies because they understand that such reform is essential to make us safer. Jonathan Powers, an Iraq war veteran and chief operating officer for the Truman National Security Project, said "We recognize that climate change is already affecting destabilized states that have fragile governments. That's why hundreds of veterans in nearly all 50 states are standing up with Operation Free—because they know that in those fragile states, against those extremist groups, it is our military that is going to have to act."

The CNA [Center for Naval Analysis] Corporation's Military Advisory Board determined in 2007 that "Climate change can act as a threat multiplier for instability in some of the most volatile regions of the world, and it presents significant national security challenges for the United States." In an update of its 2007 report last year CNA found that climate change, energy dependence, and national security are interlinked challenges.

The report, "Powering America's Defense: Energy and the Risks to National Security," reiterates the finding that fossil fuel dependence is unequivocally compromising our national security. The board concludes, "Overdependence on imported oil—by the U.S. and other nations—tethers America to unstable and hostile regimes, subverts foreign policy goals, and requires the U.S. to stretch its military presence across the globe."

CNA advises, "Given the national security threats of America's current energy posture, a major shift in energy policy and practice is required."

Profiting from the Status Quo

Many major oil companies and their trade association, the American Petroleum Institute, are some of the most vocal opponents of increasing American energy independence and reducing global warming pollution. This is likely because they profit by buying oil from "dangerous or unstable" states. This includes importing oil from Syria, Saudi Arabia, Nigeria, Mauritania, Iraq, Congo, Colombia, Chad, and Algeria.

In 2008 Chevron made a profit of $23.9 billion while nearly half of its imports—138 million barrels of oil—came from these countries. ExxonMobil made $45.2 billion while getting 43 percent of its oil—205.6 million barrels—from these countries. About one-third of BP's imports—110.6 million barrels—were from these countries in 2008, when the company's profits were $25.6 billion.

The American Petroleum Institute spent $75.2 million for public relations and advertising in 2008.

Approximately 25 percent of ConocoPhillips' imports were from "dangerous or unstable" countries—116.7 million barrels—in 2008, contributing to its $52.7 billion profit. And Shell raked in $31.4 billion that year, also importing one-quarter of its oil—61.8 million barrels—from these countries. (Note: Shell includes Shell Chemical LP, Shell Chemical Yabucoa Inc, Shell US Trading Co, Shell Oil Co, and Shell Oil Co Deer Park).

With that kind of money it's no wonder Big Oil is doing everything in its power to maintain the status quo. The companies are spending record amounts on lobbying to stop clean-energy and climate legislation. The American Petroleum Institute spent $75.2 million for public relations and advertising in 2008, and in the third quarter of 2009 the oil and gas industry outspent all other sectors lobbying on climate change, with Exxon Mobil leading the pack spending $7.2 million.

Instead of sending money abroad for oil, investing in clean-energy technology innovation would boost growth and create jobs.

Oil companies are also the main source of funding for API's front group, Energy Citizens, which makes false claims that climate change legislation will be a national energy tax and job killer. In reality, passing clean-energy and pollution reduction legislation will be affordable and even save consumers money while creating a net of 1.7 million jobs.

Clean Energy Can Help the Economy

The United States has an opportunity right now to reduce its dependence on foreign oil by adopting clean-energy and global warming pollution reduction policies that would spur economic recovery and long-term sustainable growth. With a struggling economy and record unemployment, we need that money invested here to enhance our economic competitiveness. Instead of sending money abroad for oil, investing in clean-energy technology innovation would boost growth and create jobs.

Reducing oil imports through clean-energy reform would reduce money sent overseas for oil, keep more money at home for investments, and cut global warming pollution. A Center for American Progress analysis shows that the clean-energy provisions in the American Recovery and Reinvestment Act and ACES [American Clean Energy and Security Act of 2009] combined would generate approximately $150 billion per year in new clean-energy investments over the next decade. This government-induced spending will come primarily from the private sector, and the investments would create jobs and help reduce oil dependence.

And by creating the conditions for a strong economic recovery, such as creating more finance for energy retrofits and energy-saving projects and establishing loans for manufacturing low-carbon products, we can give the United States the advantage in the clean-energy race. Investing in a clean-energy economy is the clear path toward re-establishing our economic stability and strengthening our national security.

3

Foreign Oil Dependence Is an Economic and Political Advantage

Roger Howard

Roger Howard is the author of The Oil Hunters.

While many political figures and commentators worry that oil imports leave the United States economically and militarily vulnerable, the fear is unjustified. Although the United States is dependent on foreign markets, those markets are equally dependent on the United States: if the oil is not purchased, the oil producing country suffers an economic setback. Many oil producing countries are also highly dependent on United States technology to help develop new resources. The relationship between oil producing countries and the United States also promotes peaceful relationship between countries: if a country becomes belligerent, then the United States can 1) refuse to buy oil from the country and 2) refuse to help the country develop oil resources. When all of these factors are considered, oil actually works to bring all parties together in common interest.

In its collective mindset, every nation not only harbors aspirations, fears and delusions but also conjures rogues, villains and scapegoats upon which it vents its anguish, insecurities and resentments. And for many Americans, one such villain is a highly prized commodity.

Roger Howard, "An Ode to Oil," *Wall Street Journal*, November 29, 2008. p. W1.

Oil is, after all, a primary source of man-made global warming, while spillages and drilling have sometimes inflicted lethal environmental damage. Despite the sharp falls of recent months, dramatic price rises have also underwritten every postwar global recession, including the current economic malaise.

Oil lies at the heart of bitter civil wars in several parts of the world, notably West Africa, while several governments have recently been scrambling to stake their claims over the newly discovered deposits of the Arctic. Above all, it is often regarded as America's strategic Achilles' heel. President-elect Barack Obama has promised to end U.S. "foreign oil dependency," claiming that it can be used as a "weapon" that allows overseas governments, particularly "unstable, undemocratic governments . . . to wield undue influence over America's national security." Last weekend, Mr. Obama announced his plan to create a major economic stimulus package, including spending on alternate energy.

Alarming as these scenarios are, they disguise the true picture, one that is really much more complicated and much more reassuring. While there are, of course, circumstances in which oil can exacerbate tensions and be a source of conflict, it can also act as a peacemaker and source of stability. So to identify America's "foreign oil dependency" as a source of vulnerability and weakness is just too neat and easy.

The Global Market and Oil

This identification wholly ignores the dependency of foreign oil producers on their consumers, above all on the world's largest single market—the United States. Despite efforts to diversify their economies, all of the world's key exporters are highly dependent on oil's proceeds and have always lived in fear of the moment that has now become real—when global demand slackens and prices fall. The recent, dramatic fall in price per barrel—now standing at around $54, less than four months after peaking at $147—perfectly exemplifies the producers' predicament.

So even if such a move were possible in today's global market, no oil exporter is ever in a position to alienate its customers. Supposed threats of embargoes ring hollow because no producer can assume that its own economy will be damaged any less than that of any importing country. What's more, a supply disruption would always seriously damp global demand. Even in the best of times, a prolonged price spike could easily tip the world into economic recession, prompt consumers to shake off their gasoline dependency, or accelerate a scientific drive to find alternative fuels. Fearful of this "demand destruction" when crude prices soared so spectacularly in the summer, the Saudis pledged to pump their wells at full tilt. It seems that their worst fears were realized: Americans drove 9.6 billion fewer miles in July this year compared with last, according to the Department of Transportation.

The United States has powerful political leverage over producers because it holds the key to future oil supply as well as market demand.

Instead, the dependency of foreign oil producers on their customers plays straight into America's strategic hands. Washington is conceivably in a position to hold producers to ransom by threatening to accelerate a drive to develop or implement alternative fuels, realizing the warning once uttered by Sheikh Ahmed Zaki Yamani, the former Saudi oil minister who pointed out that "the Stone Age did not end for lack of stone." Back in 1973, as they protested at Washington's stance on the Arab-Israeli dispute, Middle East producers were in a position to impose an oil embargo on the Western world. But a generation later, technological advances, and the strength of public and scientific concern about global warming, have turned the tables.

Technology and Oil

The United States has powerful political leverage over producers because it holds the key to future oil supply as well as market demand. The age of "easy oil" is over, and as fears grow that oil is becoming harder to get, so too will the dependency of producers on increasingly sophisticated Western technology and expertise.

Such skills will be particularly important in two key areas of oil production. One is finding and extracting offshore deposits, like the massive reserves reckoned to be under the Caspian and Arctic seas, or in Brazil's recently discovered Tupi field. The other is prolonging the lifespan of declining wells through enhanced "tertiary" recovery. Because Western companies have a clear technological edge over their global competitors in these hugely demanding areas, Washington exerts some powerful political leverage over exporters, many of whom openly anticipate the moment when their production peaks before gradually starting to decline.

Oil could also help the outside world frustrate the nuclear ambitions of Iran, whose output is likely to steadily decline over the coming years.

Syria illustrates how this leverage can work. Although oil has been the primary source of national income for more than 40 years, production has recently waned dramatically; Output is now nearly half of the peak it reached in the mid-1990s, when a daily output of 600,000 barrels made up 60% of gross domestic product, and can barely sustain rapidly growing domestic demand fueled by a very high rate of population growth. With enough foreign investment Syrian oil could be much more productive and enduring, but Washington has sent foreign companies, as well as American firms, a tough message to steer well clear. It is not surprising, then, that the Damascus regime regards a rapprochement with the

27

U.S. as a political lifeline and in recent months has shown signs of a new willingness to compromise.

The same predicament confronted Libya's Col. Moammar Gadhafi, who first offered to surrender weapons of mass destruction during secret negotiations with U.S. officials in May 1999. Facing a deepening economic crisis that he could not resolve without increasing the production of his main export, oil, Col. Gadhafi was prepared to bow to Washington's demands and eventually struck a path-breaking accord in December 2003. Col. Gadhafi had been the "Mad Dog" of the Reagan years, but oil's influence had initiated what President [George W.] Bush hailed as "the process of rejoining the community of nations."

Oil could also help the outside world frustrate the nuclear ambitions of Iran, whose output is likely to steadily decline over the coming years unless it has access to the latest Western technology. Many wells are aging rapidly and the Iranians cannot improve recovery rates, or exploit their new discoveries, unless Washington lifts sanctions, which have been highly successful in deterring international investment.

Oil Promotes Peace

Sometimes the markets will prove at least as effective as any American sanctions in keeping a tight political rein on oil producers. For example, when Russian forces attacked South Ossetia and Georgia on Aug. 8 [2008], Russia's stock market—of which energy stocks comprise 60%—plunged by nearly 7%, and within a week capital outflow reached a massive $16 billion, suddenly squeezing domestic credit while the ruble collapsed in value. A month later, the country was facing its worst crisis since the default of August 1998. But the future of the oil sector is so dependent on attracting massive foreign investment, and the wider Russian economy so heavily dependent on petrodollars, that the Kremlin simply can't afford to unnecessarily unnerve investors.

Today the markets know that Russia needs at least $1 trillion in investment if it is to maintain, let alone increase, its oil production. Just five years ago, output was increasing so fast—energy giants Yukos and Sibneft were posting annual production gains of 20%—that even the Saudis were worried about their own global dominance. But in the past year Russian oil production has started to wane. Leonid Fedun, a top official at Lukoil, Russia's No. 2 oil producer, admitted back in April that national output had peaked and was unlikely to return to 2007 levels "in my lifetime" and that "the period of intense oil production [growth] is over." Without foreign money and expertise to extract offshore oil and prolong the lifespan of existing wells, Russian production will fall dramatically.

Russia's oil, in other words, acted as peacemaker. This seems paradoxical for it has sometimes been said that the Kremlin's attack on South Ossetia and Georgia was prompted by an ambition to seize control of local pipelines. But although this was an aggravating factor, it was not the primary cause because Russian leaders would have felt threatened—reasonably or not—by the presence of NATO [North Atlantic Treaty Organization] in what they regard as their own backyard even if the region was not an energy hub. They were also reportedly eyeing Ukraine, which has no petroleum deposits of its own and poses no threat to the dominance of their giant energy company, Gazprom.

Oil can also act as a peacemaker and source of stability because many conflicts, in almost every part of the world, can threaten a disruption of supply and instantly send crude prices spiraling. Despite the recent price falls, the market is still vulnerable to sudden supply shocks, and a sharp increase would massively affect the wider global economy. This would have potentially disastrous social and political results, just as in the summer many countries, including France, Nepal and Indonesia, were rocked by violent protests at dramatic price increases in gasoline.

Oil and the Economy

Haunted by the specter of higher oil prices at a time of such economic fragility, many governments have a very strong incentive to use diplomacy, not force, to resolve their own disputes, and to help heal other people's. This is true not just of oil consumers but producers, which would also be keen not to watch global demand stifled by such price spikes.

Consider the events of last fall, when the Ankara government [in Turkey] was set to retaliate against the Iraq-based Kurdish guerrillas who had killed 17 Turkish soldiers and taken others prisoner in a cross-border raid on Oct. 21, 2007. Even the mere prospect of such an attack sent the price of a barrel surging to a then record high of $85 because the markets knew that the insurgents could respond by damaging a key pipeline which moves 750,000 barrels of oil across Turkish territory every day.

Oil is such a vital commodity, for consumers, producers and intermediaries alike, that it represents a meeting point for all manner of different interests.

Not surprisingly, the Bush administration pushed very hard to prevent a Turkish invasion of northern Iraq—State Department spokesman Sean McCormack aptly described the frenzy of diplomatic activity as a "full-court press"—not just to avoid shattering the vestiges of Iraq's political structure but also to stabilize oil prices. In the end it was American pressure that averted a major incursion, allowing crude prices to quickly ease. And the Turks would also have been aware that any invasion could have prompted retaliatory damage on the oil pipeline, losing them vast transit fees.

In general, oil is such a vital commodity, for consumers, producers and intermediaries alike, that it represents a meeting point for all manner of different interests. Sometimes it offers an opportunity for competitors and rivals to resolve differences, as in March 1995, when Iranian President Akbar Hashemi Rafsanjani tried to break deadlock with Washington by offering a technically very demanding oil contract to Conoco. Today, the symbiotic energy requirements of Europe and Russia allows scope to improve mutual relations, not least if European governments act in unison to impose the rules of the European Union's energy charter on Moscow. Oil also gives consumers a chance to penalize, or tempt, international miscreants, just as U.S. sanctions are forcing the Tehran regime [in Iran] to reassess its cost-benefit analysis of building the bomb.

What cannot go unchallenged is a facile equation between oil on the one hand, and war, bloodshed and, in America's particular case, strategic vulnerability on the other. For oil, fortunately, can often be our guardian.

4

Oil Dependence Strengthens US Enemies

Jonathan Powers

Jonathan Powers is the Chief Operating Officer of the Truman National Security Project.

Dependence on foreign oil has created a number of problems for the United States, the most pressing of which includes national security. Because the US imports the majority of its oil, it is forced to buy from countries that are considered dangerous by the State Department. Even when the US buys from allies, however, demand for oil drives prices higher, benefiting allies and non-allies alike. These threats speak to the need for comprehensive legislation that considers energy alternatives. These alternatives will likewise have the benefit of reducing global conflict. With military leaders arguing that the US could face dire consequences if oil consumption remains at current levels, the need to act is imminent.

The U.S. sends approximately one billion dollars a day overseas to import oil. While this figure is staggering by itself, the dangerous implications of our addiction are even more pronounced when analyzing where our money goes—and whom it helps to support.

Examine what the true costs of our oil addiction meant during the year 2008:

- *One Billion Dollars a Day Spent on Foreign Oil*: In 2008, the United States imported *4.7 billion* barrels of crude oil to meet our consumption needs. The average price per barrel of imported oil for 2008 was $92.61. This works out to *$1.19 billion per day* for the year.

- *Our Annual Oil Debt Is Greater than Our Trade Deficit with China*: Our petroleum imports created a $386 billion U.S. trade deficit in 2008, versus a $266 billion deficit with China. This national debt is a drain on our economy and an anchor on our economic growth.

- *We Overwhelmingly Rely on Oil Imports . . .*: In 2008, we consumed 7.1 billion barrels of oil in the United States, meaning that the 4.7 billion barrels of crude oil we imported was *66%* of our overall oil usage. About *one out of every six* dollars spent on imports by the U.S. is spent on oil, representing 16% of all U.S. import expenditures in 2008. According to calculations from the Center for American Progress, U.S. spending to import foreign oil amounted to 2.3% of our overall GDP in 2008.

- *. . . to the Detriment of National Security*: Vice Admiral Dennis McGinn, retired Deputy Chief of Naval Warfare Requirements and Programs, captured the national security dangers of our addiction to oil in 2009 testimony before the U.S. Senate Environment and Public Works Committee: "In 2008, we sent *$386 billion* overseas to pay for oil—much of it going to nations that wish us harm. This is an unprecedented and unsustainable transfer of wealth to other nations. It puts us in the untenable position of funding both sides of the conflict and directly undermines our fight against terror."

Our oil addiction drives up prices worldwide, pouring funds into the coffers of foreign regimes that hold anti-American sentiments, harbor terrorists, and otherwise threaten America's national security. As the Council on Foreign Relations wrote, "major energy consumers—notably the United States, but other countries as well—are finding that their growing dependence on imported energy increases their strategic vulnerability and constrains their ability to pursue a broad range of foreign policy and national security objectives."

In 2008, the U.S. imported about 4 million barrels of oil a day from countries labeled "dangerous or unstable" by the State Department.

The *one billion dollars* a day that Americans send overseas on oil floods a global oil market that enriches hostile governments, funds terrorist organizations, and props up repressive regimes. Former CIA Director Jim Woolsey explains it this way:

> "Except for our own Civil War, this [the war on terror] is the only war that we have fought where we are paying for both sides. We pay Saudi Arabia $160 billion for its oil, and $3 or $4 billion of that goes to the Wahhabis, who teach children to hate. We are paying for these terrorists with our SUVs."

A comprehensive energy strategy—one that cuts our addiction to fossil fuels, boosts clean energy technology, and moves our nation dramatically towards greater energy independence—is vital to our national security, to the safety of our men and women in uniform, and to the fight against terrorism.

A Dangerous and Unstable Addiction

While the U.S. imports 66% of our oil, that figure includes both friendly nations such as Canada and Mexico, as well as a litany of countries whose regimes are either unstable, unfriendly, or both.

In 2008, the U.S. imported about *4 million* barrels of oil a day from countries labeled "dangerous or unstable" by the State Department. Using the $386 billion total cost as cited by Vice Admiral McGinn, this means that about *39%* of our oil import costs were from "dangerous or unstable" nations.

Nearly *one-fifth* of the oil consumed by the U.S. in 2008 (18%), was imported from countries of the Middle East and Venezuela. This total represents over *one-fourth* of our overall imported oil (28%) in 2008. While Venezuela is not on the State Department's "dangerous or unstable" list, it has maintained a distinctly anti-American foreign and energy policy under President Hugo Chavez. Venezuela was one of the *top five* oil exporters to the United States, and we imported *435 million* barrels of oil from it in 2008.

Buying from Friendly Countries Doesn't Help

The price of oil is set globally. That means that even when we buy oil from friendly countries, we drive up demand, inflating prices that enrich unfriendly countries. For instance, despite U.S. laws against purchasing oil from Iran, the global demand for oil—aided by U.S. consumption habits—helps to drive up the global price of oil and line the pockets of the Iranian regime. Oil wealth funded about *60%* of the Iranian national budget in 2008. *The Economist* calculated that, in his first term, Iranian President Mahmoud Ahmadinejad benefited from "a windfall of *$250 billion* in oil sales." The United States currently consumes approximately one-fourth of the world's oil, inadvertently bolstering Iran's bottom line, despite the laws on the books.

All oil demand hurts our national security—regardless of whether the oil is produced here at home or bought overseas. Whether oil is directly purchased from nations on the State Department's "Dangerous or Unstable" list, or is bought from West Texas, U.S. demand increases global oil prices that fund our enemies.

According to testimony from Truman National Security Project Chief Operating Officer Jonathan Powers, every $5 increase in the global price of crude oil represents:

- An additional *$7.9 billion* for Iran and President Ahmadinejad;

- An additional *$4.7 billion* for Venezuela and President Chavez; and,

- An additional *$18 billion* for Russia and Prime Minister Vladimir Putin.

Depending on oil to produce the energy that runs our nation makes America vulnerable, while simultaneously providing enormous resources to those who would do us harm.

Unfortunately, even if we buy oil from a friendly country like Mexico, problem countries in the Middle East can hold us hostage by forcing up global oil prices—as Middle Eastern countries in OPEC [Organization of the Petroleum Exporting Countries] have done time and time again. Buying from friendly or domestic sources does not solve our problem, because the countries with the greatest reserves—notably, Saudi Arabia—are such major producers that they set the global supply. Even if we drilled in every untapped well in America, we simply do not have enough oil from friendly countries and under the earth at home to offset OPEC's power. By staying addicted to oil, regardless of where we purchase it, we give OPEC countries the power to cripple our economy and bring America to its knees.

A Better Alternative

Depending on oil to produce the energy that runs our nation makes America vulnerable, while simultaneously providing enormous resources to those who would do us harm. It is time for us to take control of our energy future, cut our dependence on oil, and defund terrorist threats with comprehensive energy legislation.

National security, military, and intelligence experts have spoken out about the need for a comprehensive strategy that takes on the destabilizing effects of fossil fuel dependence and global climate change.

"Without bold action now to significantly reduce our dependence on fossil fuels, our national security will be at greater risk," testified Vice Admiral Dennis McGinn, before a U.S. Senate panel. "Fierce global competition and conflict over dwindling supplies of fossil fuel will be a major part of the future strategic landscape."

"Moving toward clean, independent, domestic energy choices lessens that danger and significantly helps us confront the serious challenge of global climate change. Because these issues are so closely linked, solutions to one affect the other. Technologies and practices that improve energy sources and efficiency also reduce carbon intensity and carbon emissions, and, most critically, increase our national security."

A panel of 11 former generals and admirals echoed Vice Admiral McGinn's testimony in a report entitled *National Security and the Threat of Climate Change*, stating, "Climate change, national security, and energy dependence are a related set of global challenges ... dependence on foreign oil leaves us more vulnerable to hostile regimes and terrorists, and clean domestic energy alternatives help us confront the serious challenge of global climate change."

Marine General James Mattis put it more succinctly when he was asked at a Brookings [Institution] meeting in 2007 about the most important area of research for aiding the men and women under his command: "Unleash us from the tether of fuel."

Just as the military is innovating its own energy habits, America as a nation must do the same.

The Threat to Global Warming

America's military leaders are not waiting to take action on the threats posed by our dependence on fossil fuels. The Defense Department considers climate change such a strategic threat that it is part of the military's long term planning. The CIA has opened a center to track the threat of climate change. The Army, Navy, Air Force and the Marines have all committed to reducing their carbon pollution.

For example, in October 2009 the Navy launched the *USS Makin Island*, a first-of-its-kind hybrid powered amphibious assault vehicle that emits less carbon and saved the Navy $2 million in fuel costs during its maiden voyage alone. The Marine Corps has even created a model Forward Operating Base (FOB) in Quantico, VA, which will allow the Marines to test a hybrid power station that is set to be deployed in Afghanistan by mid-2010.

Just as the military is innovating its own energy habits, America as a nation must do the same, with a comprehensive approach to clean energy and climate change that will have a measurable impact on these threats.

The need is immediate. "We have less than ten years to change our fossil fuel dependency course in significant ways," testified Vice Admiral McGinn. "Our nation's security depends on the swift, serious, and thoughtful response to the inter-linked challenges of energy security and climate change."

5

The United States Should Reduce Its Oil Dependence

President Barack Obama

President Barack Obama is the 44th President of the United States.

Speaking at Georgetown University, President Obama outlined a new energy policy to help reduce imported oil. Unfortunately, there are no easy solutions. Overall, the US will have to rely on a variety of strategies to reduce oil dependence. That will mean increasing oil production in the US and developing alternative fuel sources, such as biofuels. Furthermore, American automobile manufacturers will have to increase fuel efficiency standards while the American people will have to reduce household energy use. While the obstacles ahead will be tremendous, the American people are capable of rising to the challenge.

We meet here at a tumultuous time for the world. In a matter of months, we've seen regimes toppled. We've seen democracy take root in North Africa and in the Middle East. We've witnessed a terrible earthquake, a catastrophic tsunami, a nuclear emergency that has battered one of our strongest allies and closest friends in the world's third-largest economy. We've led an international effort in Libya to prevent a massacre and maintain stability throughout the broader region.

And as Americans, we're heartbroken by the lives that have been lost as a result of these events. We're deeply moved by the thirst for freedom in so many nations, and we're moved by the strength and the perseverance of the Japanese people. And it's natural, I think, to feel anxious about what all of this means for us.

In an economy that relies so heavily on oil, rising prices at the pump affect everybody.

And one big area of concern has been the cost and security of our energy. Obviously, the situation in the Middle East implicates our energy security. The situation in Japan leads us to ask questions about our energy sources.

In an economy that relies so heavily on oil, rising prices at the pump affect everybody—workers, farmers, truck drivers, restaurant owners, students who are lucky enough to have a car. Businesses see rising prices at the pump hurt their bottom line. Families feel the pinch when they fill up their tank. And for Americans that are already struggling to get by, a hike in gas prices really makes their lives that much harder. It hurts.

If you're somebody who works in a relatively low-wage job and you've got to commute to work, it takes up a big chunk of your income. You may not be able to buy as many groceries. You may have to cut back on medicines in order to fill up the gas tank. So this is something that everybody is affected by.

There Are No Quick Fixes

Now, here's the thing—we have been down this road before. Remember, it was just three years ago that gas prices topped $4 a gallon. I remember because I was in the middle of a presidential campaign. Working folks certainly remember because it hit a lot of people pretty hard. And because we were at the height of political season, you had all kinds of slogans and gimmicks and outraged politicians—they were waving their three-point plans for $2 a gallon gas. You remember that—"drill, baby, drill"—and we were going through all that. And none of it was really going to do anything to solve the problem. There was a lot of hue and cry, a lot of fulminating and hand-wringing, but nothing actually happened. Imagine that in Washington.

The truth is, none of these gimmicks, none of these slogans made a bit of difference. When gas prices finally did fall, it was mostly because the global recession had led to less demand for oil. Companies were producing less; the demand for petroleum went down; prices went down. Now that the economy is recovering, demand is back up. Add the turmoil in the Middle East, and it's not surprising that oil prices are higher. And every time the price of a barrel of oil on the world market rises by $10, a gallon of gas goes up by about 25 cents.

There are no quick fixes. Anybody who tells you otherwise isn't telling you the truth.

The point is the ups and downs in gas prices historically have tended to be temporary. But when you look at the long-term trends, there are going to be more ups in gas prices than downs in gas prices. And that's because you've got countries like India and China that are growing at a rapid clip, and as 2 billion more people start consuming more goods—they want cars just like we've got cars; they want to use energy to make their lives a little easier just like we've got—it is absolutely certain that demand will go up a lot faster than supply. It's just a fact.

So here's the bottom line: There are no quick fixes. Anybody who tells you otherwise isn't telling you the truth. And we will keep on being a victim to shifts in the oil market until we finally get serious about a long-term policy for a secure, affordable energy future. . . .

US Oil Dependence

Now, here's a source of concern, though. We've known about the dangers of our oil dependence for decades. Richard Nixon talked about freeing ourselves from dependence on foreign oil. And every President since that time has talked about freeing ourselves from dependence on foreign oil. Politicians of every stripe have promised energy independence, but that promise has so far gone unmet.

I talked about reducing America's dependence on oil when I was running for President, and I'm proud of the historic progress that we've made over the last two years towards that goal, and we'll talk about that a little bit. But I've got to be honest. We've run into the same political gridlock, the same inertia that has held us back for decades.

That has to change. That has to change. We cannot keep going from shock when gas prices go up to trance when they go back down—we go back to doing the same things we've been doing until the next time there's a price spike, and then we're shocked again. We can't rush to propose action when gas prices are high and then hit the snooze button when they fall again. We can't keep on doing that.

The United States of America cannot afford to bet our long-term prosperity, our long-term security on a resource that will eventually run out, and even before it runs out will get more and more expensive to extract from the ground. We can't afford it when the costs to our economy, our country, and our planet are so high. Not when your generation needs us to get this right. It's time to do what we can to secure our energy future.

Reducing Oil Imports

And today, I want to announce a new goal, one that is reasonable, one that is achievable, and one that is necessary.

When I was elected to this office, America imported 11 million barrels of oil a day. By a little more than a decade from now, we will have cut that by one-third. That is something that we can achieve. (Applause.) We can cut our oil dependence—we can cut our oil dependence by a third.

I set this goal knowing that we're still going to have to import some oil. It will remain an important part of our energy portfolio for quite some time, until we've gotten alternative energy strategies fully in force. And when it comes to the oil we import from other nations, obviously we've got to look at neighbors like Canada and Mexico that are stable and steady and reliable sources. We also have to look at other countries like Brazil. Part of the reason I went down there is to talk about energy with the Brazilians. They recently discovered significant new oil reserves, and we can share American technology and know-how with them as they develop these resources.

But our best opportunities to enhance our energy security can be found in our own backyard—because we boast one critical, renewable resource that the rest of the world can't match: American ingenuity. American ingenuity, American know-how.

To make ourselves more secure, to control our energy future, we're going to have to harness all of that ingenuity. It's a task we won't be finished with by the end of my presidency, or even by the end of the next presidency. But if we continue the work that we've already begun over the last two years, we won't just spark new jobs, industries and innovations—we will leave your generation and future generations with a country that is safer, that is healthier, and that's more prosperous.

So today, my administration is releasing a Blueprint for a Secure Energy Future that outlines a comprehensive national energy policy, one that we've been pursuing since the day I took office. And cutting our oil dependence by a third is part of that plan. . . .

Now, meeting the goal of cutting our oil dependence depends largely on two things: first, finding and producing more oil at home; second, reducing our overall dependence on oil with cleaner alternative fuels and greater efficiency.

Increasing America's Oil Supply

This begins by continuing to increase America's oil supply. Even for those of you who are interested in seeing a reduction in our dependence on fossil fuels—and I know how passionate young people are about issues like climate change—the fact of the matter is, is that for quite some time, America is going to be still dependent on oil in making its economy work.

Now, last year, American oil production reached its highest level since 2003. And for the first time in more than a decade, oil we imported accounted for less than half of the liquid fuel we consumed. So that was a good trend. To keep reducing that reliance on imports, my administration is encouraging offshore oil exploration and production—as long as it's safe and responsible.

I don't think anybody here has forgotten what happened last year, where we had to deal with the largest oil spill in [our] history. I know some of the fishermen down in the Gulf Coast haven't forgotten it. And what we learned from that disaster helped us put in place smarter standards of safety and responsibility. For example, if you're going to drill in deepwater, you've got to prove before you start drilling that you can actually contain an underwater spill. That's just common sense. And lately, we've been hearing folks saying, well, the Obama administration, they put restrictions on how oil companies operate offshore. Well, yes, because we just spent all that time, energy and money trying to clean up a big mess. And I don't know about you, but I don't have amnesia. I remember these things. And I think it was important for us to make sure that we prevent something like that from happening again. (Applause.)

Now, today, we're working to expedite new drilling permits for companies that meet these higher standards. Since they were put in, we've approved 39 new shallow-water permits; we've approved seven deepwater permits in recent weeks. When it comes to drilling offshore, my administration approved more than two permits last year for every new well that the industry started to drill. So any claim that my administration is responsible for gas prices because we've "shut down" oil production, any claim like that is simply untrue. It might make for a useful sound bite, but it doesn't track with reality.

What is true is we've said if you're going to drill offshore you've got to have a plan to make sure that we don't have the kind of catastrophe that we had last year. And I don't think that there's anybody who should dispute that that's the right strategy to pursue.

Producing more oil in America can help lower oil prices, can help create jobs, and can enhance our energy security.

Moreover, we're actually pushing the oil industry to take advantage of the opportunities that they've already got. Right now the industry holds tens of millions of acres of leases where they're not producing a single drop. They're just sitting on supplies of American energy that are ready to be tapped. That's why part of our plan is to provide new and better incentives that promote rapid, responsible development of these resources.

We're also exploring and assessing new frontiers for oil and gas development from Alaska to the Mid- and South Atlantic states, because producing more oil in America can help lower oil prices, can help create jobs, and can enhance our energy security, but we've got to do it in the right way.

Alternative Fuel Sources

Now, even if we increase domestic oil production, that is not going to be the long-term solution to our energy challenge. I give out this statistic all the time, and forgive me for repeating it again: America holds about 2 percent of the world's proven oil reserves. What that means is, is that even if we drilled every drop of oil out of every single one of the reserves that we possess—offshore and onshore—it still wouldn't be enough to meet our long-term needs. We consume about 25 percent of the world's oil. We only have 2 percent of the reserves. Even if we doubled U.S. oil production, we're still really short.

So the only way for America's energy supply to be truly secure is by permanently reducing our dependence on oil. We're going to have to find ways to boost our efficiency so we use less oil. We've got to discover and produce cleaner, renewable sources of energy that also produce less carbon pollution, which is threatening our climate. And we've got to do it quickly.

Now, in terms of new sources of energy, we have a few different options. The first is natural gas. Recent innovations have given us the opportunity to tap large reserves—perhaps a century's worth of reserves, a hundred years worth of reserves—in the shale under our feet. But just as is true in terms of us extracting oil from the ground, we've got to make sure that we're extracting natural gas safely, without polluting our water supply.

That's why I've asked Secretary [Steven] Chu, my Energy Secretary, to work with other agencies, the natural gas industry, states, and environmental experts to improve the safety of this process. And Chu is the right guy to do this. He's got a Nobel Prize in physics. He actually deserved his Nobel Prize. And this is the kind of thing that he likes to do for fun on the weekend. He goes into his garage and he tinkers around and figures out how to extract natural gas.

I'm going to embarrass him further. Last year, when we were trying to fill—figure out how to close the cap, I sent Chu down to sit in the BP [British Petroleum] offices, and he essentially designed the cap that ultimately worked, and he drew up the specs for it and had BP build it, construct it. So this is somebody who knows what he's doing. So for those of you who are studying physics, it may actually pay off someday.

But the potential for natural gas is enormous. . . .

Biofuels

Now, another substitute for oil that holds tremendous promise is renewable biofuels—not just ethanol, but biofuels made from things like switchgrass and wood chips and biomass.

If anybody doubts the potential of these fuels, consider Brazil. As I said, I was just there last week. Half of Brazil's vehicles can run on biofuels—half of their fleet of automobiles can run on biofuels instead of petroleum. Just last week, our Air Force—our own Air Force—used an advanced biofuel blend to fly a Raptor 22—an F-22 Raptor faster than the speed of sound. Think about that. I mean, if an F-22 Raptor can fly at the speed of—faster than the speed of sound on biomass, then I know the old beater that you've got, that you're driving around in—can probably do so, too. There's no reason why we can't have our cars do the same.

There's no reason we shouldn't be using these renewable fuels throughout America.

In fact, the Air Force is aiming to get half of its domestic jet fuel from alternative sources by 2016. And I'm directing the Navy and the Department of Energy and Agriculture to work with the private sector to create advanced biofuels that can power not just fighter jets, but also trucks and commercial airliners.

So there's no reason we shouldn't be using these renewable fuels throughout America. And that's why we're investing in things like fueling stations and research into the next generation of biofuels. One of the biggest problems we have with alternative energy is not just producing the energy, but also distributing it. We've got gas stations all around the country, so whenever you need gas you know you can fill up—it doesn't matter where you are. Well, we've got to have that same kind of distribution network when it comes to our renewable energy sources so that when you are converting to a different kind of car that runs on a different kind of energy, you're going to be able to have that same convenience. Otherwise, the market won't work; it won't grow.

Over the next two years, we'll help entrepreneurs break ground for four next-generation biorefineries—each with a capacity of more than 20 million gallons per year. And going forward, we should look for ways to reform biofuels incentives to make sure that they're meeting today's challenges and that they're also saving taxpayers money.

So as we replace oil with fuels like natural gas and biofuels, we can also reduce our dependence by making cars and trucks that use less oil in the first place. Seventy percent of our petroleum consumption goes to transportation—70 percent. And by the way, so does the second biggest chunk of most families' budgets goes into transportation. And that's why one of the best ways to make our economy less dependent on oil and save folks more money is to make our transportation sector more efficient.

Fuel Efficient Standards

Now, we went through 30 years where we didn't raise fuel efficiency standards on cars. And part of what happened in the U.S. auto industry was because oil appeared relatively cheap, the U.S. auto industry decided we're just going to make our money on SUVs, and we're not going to worry about fuel efficiency. Thirty years of lost time when it comes to technology that could improve the efficiency of cars.

So last year, we established a groundbreaking national fuel efficiency standard for cars and trucks. We did this last year without legislation. We just got all the parties together and we got them to agree—automakers, autoworkers, environmental groups, industry.

So that means our cars will be getting better gas mileage, saving 1.8 billion barrels of oil over the life of the program— 1.8 billion. Our consumers will save money from fewer trips to the pump—$3,000 on average over time you will save because of these higher fuel efficiency standards. And our automakers will build more innovative products. Right now, there are even cars rolling off the assembly lines in Detroit with combustion engines—I'm not talking about hybrids—combustion engines that get more than 50 miles per gallon. So we know how to do it. We know how to make our cars more efficient.

But going forward, we're going to continue to work with the automakers, with the autoworkers, with states, to ensure the high-quality, fuel-efficient cars and trucks of tomorrow are built right here in the United States of America. That's going to be a top priority for us.

This summer, we're going to propose the first-ever fuel efficiency standards for heavy-duty trucks. And this fall, we'll announce the next round of fuel standards for cars that builds on what we've already done.

And by the way, the federal government is going to need to lead by example. The fleet of cars and trucks we use in the federal government is one of the largest in the country. We've got a lot of cars. And that's why we've already doubled the number of alternative vehicles in the federal fleet. And that's why today I am directing agencies to purchase 100 percent alternative fuel, hybrid, or electric vehicles by 2015. All of them should be alternative fuel.

Other Fuel Saving Projects

Going forward, we'll partner with private companies that want to upgrade their large fleets. And this means, by the way, that you students, as consumers or future consumers of cars, you've got to make sure that you are boosting demand for alternative vehicles. You're going to have a responsibility as well, because if alternative-fuel vehicles are manufactured but you guys aren't buying them, then folks will keep on making cars that don't have the same fuel efficiency. So you've got power in this process, and the decisions you make individually in your lives will say something about how serious we are when it comes to energy independence.

We've also made historic investments in high-speed rail and mass transit, because part of making our transportation sector cleaner and more efficient involves offering all Americans, whether they are urban, suburban, or rural, the choice to be mobile without having to get in a car and pay for gas.

Still, there are few breakthroughs as promising for increasing fuel efficiency and reducing our dependence on oil as electric vehicles. Soon after I took office, I set a goal of having one million electric vehicles on our roads by 2015. We've created incentives for American companies to develop these vehicles, and for Americans who want them to buy them.

So new manufacturing plants are opening over the next few years. And a modest $2 billion investment in competitive grants for companies to develop the next generation of batteries for these cars has jumpstarted a big new American industry. Pretty soon, America will be home to 40 percent of global manufacturing capacity for these advanced batteries.

And for those of you who are wondering what that means, the thing that's been holding back electric vehicles is the battery that stores that electricity, that energy. And the more efficient, the more lightweight we can make those batteries, the easier it is to manufacture those cars at a competitive price.

And if we can have that industry here in the United States of America, that means jobs. If those batteries are made here, the cars are made here. Those cars are made here, we're putting Americans back to work.

Now, to make sure we stay on this goal we're going to need to do more—by offering more powerful incentives to consumers, and by rewarding the communities that pave the way for the adoption of these vehicles.

Now, one other thing about electric cars—and you don't need to talk to Chu about this—it turns out electric cars run on electricity. And so even if we reduce our oil dependency, and we're producing all these great electric cars, we're going to have to have a plan to change the way we generate electricity in America so that it's cleaner and safer and healthier. We know that ushering in a clean energy economy has the potential of creating untold numbers of new jobs and new businesses right here in the United States. But we're going to have to think about how do we produce electricity more efficiently.

Homes and businesses consume 40 percent of the energy that we use, and it costs us billions of dollars in energy bills.

Reducing Household Energy Use

Now, in addition to producing it, we actually also have to think about making sure we're not wasting energy.... Every institution and every household has to start thinking about how are we reducing the amount of energy that we're using and doing it in more efficient ways.

Today, our homes and businesses consume 40 percent of the energy that we use, and it costs us billions of dollars in energy bills. Manufacturers that require large amounts of energy to make their products, they're challenged by rising energy costs. And so you can't separate the issue of oil dependence from the issue of how we are producing generally—more energy generally.

And that's why we've proposed new programs to help Americans upgrade their homes and businesses and plants with new, energy-efficient building materials—new lighting, new windows, new heating and cooling systems—investments that will save consumers and business owners tens of billions of dollars a year, and free up money for investment and hiring and creating new jobs and hiring more workers and putting contractors to work as well.

The nice thing about energy efficiency is we already have the technology. We don't have to create something new. We just have to help businesses and homeowners put in place the installation, the energy-efficient windows, the energy-efficient lighting. They'll get their money back. You will save money on your electricity bill that pays for those improvements that you made, but a lot of people may not have the money up front, and so we've got to give them some incentives to do that.

And just like the fuels we use in our cars, we're going to have to find cleaner renewable sources of electricity. Today, about two-fifths of our electricity come from clean energy sources. But we can do better than that. I think that with the right incentives in place, we can double our use of clean energy. And that's why, in my State of the Union address back in January [2011], I called for a new Clean Energy Standard for America: By 2035, 80 percent of our electricity needs to come from a wide range of clean energy sources—renewables like wind and solar, efficient natural gas. And, yes, we're going to have to examine how do we make clean coal and nuclear power work. . . .

The Challenge Ahead

Let me close by speaking directly to the students here—the next generation who are going to be writing the next great chapter in the American story. The issue of energy independence is one that America has been talking about since before your parents were your age, since before you were born. And you also happen to go to a school [in a town] that for a long time has suffered from a chronic unwillingness to come together and make tough choices. And so I forgive you for thinking that maybe there isn't much we can do to rise to this challenge. Maybe some of you are feeling kind of cynical or skeptical about whether we're actually going to solve this problem. But everything I have seen and experienced with your generation convinces me otherwise.

I think that precisely because you are coming of age at a time of such rapid and sometimes unsettling change, born into a world with fewer walls, educated in an era of constant information, tempered by war and economic turmoil—because that's the world in which you're coming of age, I think you believe as deeply as any of our previous generations that America can change and it can change for the better.

We need that. We need you to dream big. We need you to summon that same spirit of unbridled optimism and that bold willingness to tackle tough challenges and see those challenges through that led previous generations to rise to greatness—to save a democracy, to touch the moon, to connect the world with our own science and our own imagination.

That's what America is capable of. That's what you have to push America to do, and it will be you that pushes it. That history of ours, of meeting challenges—that's your birthright. You understand that there's no problem out there that is not within our power to solve.

I don't want to leave this challenge for future Presidents. I don't want to leave it for my children. I don't want to leave it for your children. So, yes, solving it will take time and it will take effort. It will require our brightest scientists, our most creative companies. It will require all of us—Democrats, Republicans, and everybody in between—to do our part. But with confidence in America and in ourselves and in one another, I know this is a challenge that we will solve.

6

A Broad-Based Solution to Our Energy Problem

Ben Adler

Ben Adler writes for the Nation, Newsweek, *and* American Prospect.

While President Obama has attempted to address America's reliance on foreign oil, his solutions have been predictable. With a focus on energy policy, he has failed to understand that other progressive domestic policies are needed to curb oil imports. In transportation, for instance, the US has continued to build new highways as opposed to high-speed rail; likewise, taxes on gasoline have remained low, further encouraging Americans to use cars for all transportation. Similar policies encourage building new homes, which creates urban sprawl. If the President wishes to truly decrease oil imports, he should enact reforms that help Americans reduce the daily use of energy.

The real solutin to our oil-consumption problem won't be solved by energy policy.

With instability in the Arab world causing oil prices to surge, and Republicans proposing, with typical venality and idiocy, to solve the problem through either rampant domestic oil drilling or stealing the oil in Iraq and Libya, President Barack Obama is striking a more reasoned tone. In a recent speech at Georgetown University, the president proposed reducing America's foreign oil imports by one-third by 2025. In itself, this sounds like a worthy goal, but given the breadth of the environmental and economic problems that our oil consumption causes, it's unambitious at best.

Part of the problem is that Obama's approach is entirely conventional. He calls for reductions in oil use through boosting alternative-energy sources like natural gas and biofuels and increasing domestic oil production. This shows a fatal flaw in Obama's conception of the problem. He views our massive oil consumption as an issue that should be solved through energy policy. In fact, the real solutions to our energy problems lie in other policy areas: transportation, education, housing, and urban development.

The U.S. has unwisely encouraged development patterns that forced us to drive everywhere and to drive longer distances.

When Republicans chant "drill baby, drill" and the country's leading Democrat responds with "drill but also build solar panels" as an opening offer rather than a final compromise, the whole debate is skewed rightward. Our reliance on oil is a problem caused by excessive demand, not inadequate supply. The way to solve such a problem is not to scurry in vain to produce enough oil to match demand—an exercise akin to running in quicksand—but to reduce demand. And to do that requires changing rules that no president has ever identified as falling under energy policy at all.

Our rapacious oil consumption results from decisions made long ago, especially when it comes to transportation. According to the World Resources Institute, in 2005 the U.S. consumed 1,618.6 litres of petroleum per person; Japan and Germany—two nations with robust automobile industries— used around a quarter of that per person compared with the U.S. It's not that Americans can't enjoy the benefits of building or owning cars but the U.S. has unwisely encouraged development patterns that forced us to drive everywhere and to drive longer distances.

Because of this, the U.S. has set lower taxes on gasoline compared to other developed nations, and we use the revenue to build roads—about 80 percent of federal transportation dollars go to highways—rather than subways and regional rail lines. We need to raise the federal gas tax, which hasn't even risen to keep pace with inflation since 1993, and reapportion the way we spend that revenue.

Housing policy, too, needs to change. Supporting consumer spending on buying a new home instead of renting or rehabilitating an older home in the inner-city has led to suburban sprawl. Not only does this mean people drive more and drive farther but that they live in detached houses and work in suburban office parks and strip malls, all of which consume more energy than apartment buildings, town houses, and urban skyscrapers. We need to stop favoring new homeownership over renting (via the mortgage interest tax deduction and other subsidies). Decreasing the emphasis on homeownership and single-family home development will have the added benefits of preventing future housing bubbles and increasing socioeconomic and racial integration.

Middle-class families are also lured to the suburbs by education policies that allow those schools to be so much better than the ones in inner cities. Whereas many countries finance schools largely through general revenues at the national or regional level, the U.S. leaves most school funding up to localities, which often rely largely on property taxes. The result? Suburban school districts have more advantaged populations and better resources. Most suburban students rely on school buses or cars to get to school. This, of course, uses more oil than walking and the cost of all that gas guzzling has become a major problem for districts struggling with rising gas prices. But the bigger problem is that the socioeconomically segregated schools create inequality of opportunity and, from a land-use perspective, this means that middle-class families will keep leaving the city to give their children a better chance in life. If we raised state and federal income taxes and provisioned funding more equally across districts and also created regional mega-districts to integrate suburban and urban school districts, we could remove this incentive for white flight and suburban sprawl.

Unlike domestic drilling or subsidizing the construction of nuclear reactors, these policies do not risk catastrophic accidents. The "all of the above" approach to energy independence Obama advocates also raises the risks of future disasters like the BP oil spill. As a report released today by the NAACP to commemorate the one-year anniversary of the spill illustrates, the economic, health, and environmental impact on Gulf-area residents is still devastating and prevalent. April 2010 also featured the Massey coal mine explosion in West Virginia and a deadly accident at a coal mine in Kentucky. As a new report from the Center for American Progress demonstrates, fossil-fuel extraction is among the most dangerous industries for workers.

In theory, the best way to reduce our consumption of fossil fuels across all sectors of the economy would be to put a price or tax on carbon emissions and let the market sort out which are the best sectors to find efficiencies. With Republicans controlling the House of Representatives, though, that will not happen. But fiscal conservatives should in theory be amenable to removing market-distorting subsidies. On the federal level, those include subsidies in the tax code for fossil-fuel production, our disproportionate funding of highways over mass transit, and federal policies that subsidize buying a new home but not renting or renovating an existing home in the inner city. In fact, Obama favors many of these positions: He has released a forward-looking model for reauthorization of the Surface Transportation Act, proposed expanded high-speed rail, and endorsed removing tax expenditures like the home mortgage deduction. But Obama has not made any of these a political priority, letting the overdue Surface Transit reauthorization languish and accepting cuts to high-speed rail in the 2011 budget compromise. Most important, Obama has left these ideas in their respective silos—tax expenditures are tax policy, rail is transportation policy—instead of calling them what they are: a plan to reduce our dependence on oil.

Unfortunately, when it comes to combating the real reasons for our oil dependency, Obama has yet to bring any of them to bear.

Some of the other elements of combating suburban sprawl—such as integrating and equalizing funding between school districts and changing local zoning codes that currently require parking lots, low-density construction, and segregated uses—are largely not within the president's control. Others are within his authority, but he has avoided endorsing those policies—such as increasing the tax on gasoline to fund mass-transit priorities—which are, admittedly, political nonstarters with a Republican House of Representatives.

But our consumption of fossil fuels and its malign effects—climate change, the Gulf oil spill, worker deaths, the distorting effects on our foreign policy, and the tax we pay to hostile foreign governments—is the single biggest problem our nation faces. To address such a sprawling problem requires leadership, political courage, and outside-the-box thinking. In winning election and passing health-care reform, President Obama showed he has all those qualities. Unfortunately, when it comes to combating the real reasons for our oil dependency, Obama has yet to bring any of them to bear.

7

The US Should Seek Energy Resilience by Shifting to Electricity

Andy Grove

Andy Grove was the chairman and chief executive officer of Intel Corporation.

America's reliance on imported oil has created multiple economic and energy problems. The US must have oil for its economy to grow, but at the same time, it remains dependent on other countries for that oil supply. While many presidents have set a goal of energy independence, all have fallen far short. Instead of seeking energy independence, the US should seek energy resilience; instead of relying on imported oil, the US needs to develop energy sources at home. The new strategy will rely more heavily on electricity, which can be developed from multiple sources. Transportation, for instance, can benefit from electric cars along with dual-powered cars (electricity and gasoline). Replacing fossil fuels with electricity also has the advantage of reducing environmental problems such as global warming. As more countries struggle with dwindling oil supplies, it will be increasingly important to find a workable energy replacement. Electricity offers the best solution.

Twenty-five years ago, when I was CEO of Intel, I had an unusual experience while visiting a customer. It was during a period of tight availability of microprocessors, our main product. This was not an unusual state of affairs. Supply and demand ebbed and flowed as the computer business had its ups and downs. Sometimes we had too many chips sitting in inventory; other times, like this one, we had too few. My main purpose in visiting was to reassure the customer that we were working hard to boost production and that relief was on the way.

A strange sight greeted me as I entered the lobby. A large group of employees was waiting, standing around in a semi-circle, with the CEO, an old friend, in the center—on his knees. The employees behind him held up a sign that said, "Please feed the chip monster. He is very hungry."

Our standing in the world of oil has fallen a long way in a short time.

As flashbulbs popped, I realized the purpose of this setup. We were the sole supplier of the microprocessor this customer needed, and my promises and apologies were not going to help much. The staging was done in good spirit, but I felt deeply embarrassed—which may be why I remember the scene so vividly, even after all these years.

The episode came to mind earlier this year when I read about President Bush's visit to Saudi Arabia. His main mission was to ask the Saudis for greater petroleum output. According to press reports, his request was unceremoniously rejected by the oil minister, who did not even appear to be embarrassed. Such an exchange would have been inconceivable as recently as a decade ago. Our standing in the world of oil has fallen a long way in a short time.

Oil and Economic Growth

In fact, we may be at a critical juncture, the kind that can creep up, in a gradual and insidious way, on companies and industries, and even on societies. Invariably, the actions that are needed to change course at such times are painful. Leaders rarely appreciate the gravity of their situation, and even when they do, they are loath to take appropriate action.

After World War II, the United States was the global leader in the production and distribution of energy. In time, other countries rebuilt their war-ravaged economies. As their oil consumption increased, our prominence, both on the demand and the supply side, was gradually diluted. Our relative decline accelerated in the 1970s, after the Organization of Petroleum Exporting Countries (OPEC) was formed and then again when it flexed its muscles by precipitating the oil shock. Later, in the early 1990s, some of the developing Asian economies started to grow at a rapid rate, requiring a prodigious amount of petroleum.

Consequently, our significance as a customer started to decline in the same manner as our significance as a supplier did earlier.

The availability of petroleum may well determine whether an economy grows or declines.

Let's put this situation in perspective. Google's share of the U.S search market is more than half. This allows the firm to wield tremendous influence over the very nature of the American advertising market. Google may even have the power to transform and redefine how advertising is carried out. OPEC has a similarly dominant share of the worldwide oil market, and it may have a correspondingly large influence on its customers.

But the stages on which Google and OPEC play are dramatically different. Advertising is a big and important business, but energy is the lifeblood of all economies. Like drinking water or oxygen, we simply cannot be without it. So a supplier of energy can have significant control over customers—even nations.

The availability of petroleum may well determine whether an economy grows or declines. You can see this striking relationship by comparing the rise of China's economy with the rise in its demand for petroleum. The availability of petroleum can determine employment levels, which, in turn, for a nation like China, can determine national political stability.

The Goal That Failed

As America's energy situation began to change, so did our official energy strategy. In the early 1970s, President Nixon kicked off Project Independence, defining a national goal in his State of the Union address: "At the end of this decade, in the year 1980, the United States will not be dependent on any other country for the energy we need to provide our jobs, to heat our homes, and to keep our transportation moving."

The failure to meet that goal was dramatic.

After Nixon, president after president set similar goals. Every target was missed. We became more and more dependent on imported petroleum. Net energy imports doubled between 1970 and 1980, and then again by 1990.

Not only did America fail to meet the goals, but the goals themselves were unwise. A faulty goal leads to the wrong actions; so even if we execute flawlessly, we fail.

What was wrong with energy independence? As the decades progressed, the United States became more and more integrated into a global economy, where goods, information, and oil move unimpeded across national boundaries. Countries around the world produce energy if they can, and buy on the world market what they need beyond their own production. Oil flows toward the highest bidder, just like all other goods. Consequently, talking about "independence" in terms of one product in an otherwise seamless global economy is a contradiction. As national policy, we must protect the U.S. economy from interruptions in the supply of such a critical commodity—whether those interruptions are related to natural or political causes. I believe that the appropriate aim is to strengthen our ability to adjust to such changes—to strengthen our energy resilience.

We can do that by increasing our reliance on electricity.

Equally important is the fact that electricity can be produced from using multiple sources of energy

---

Electricity: Energy That Sticks

Oil moves to the highest bidder. Fleets of tankers carry it across oceans day and night. Natural gas can also move around, but with extra difficulties. On land, it can be transported in pipelines, but to carry it across oceans requires liquefaction and expensive, high-tech ships that can carry this liquid in strong, deeply cooled containers.

Electricity can be transported only over land. In other words, it is "sticky": it stays in the continent where it is produced.

Equally important is the fact that electricity can be produced using multiple sources of energy. Petroleum, yes—but also coal, which is abundant in the United States, wind, hydroelectric, nuclear, and solar. Electricity is a multi-sourced form of energy. If one source suffers a shortage, we can produce electricity from another.

Because electricity is the stickiest form of energy, and because it is multi-sourced, it will give us the greatest degree of energy resilience. Our nation will be best served if we dedicate ourselves to increasing the amount of our energy that we use in the form of electricity.

Transportation: The Hardest Nut to Crack

We live in a world where just about everything—from a hairdryer to the Internet—runs on electricity. A big exception is the transportation sector, critical to the movement of people, production materials, food, and even fuel. Transportation uses more than half of all the petroleum consumed in this country. If we don't convert a large portion of the transportation sector to electricity, we cannot make real progress toward energy resilience.

This conversion will not be easy. It requires substantial growth in generation capacity as well as in the capacity and reach of the transmission infrastructure. Most importantly, it requires that vehicles be able to run on electric power.

This is a very difficult technical task. With the size and weight of ordinary automobiles, current technology allows electric cars to run only 100 miles or so before their batteries need to be recharged—the way we recharge our laptop computers or cell phones, by plugging them into the national electric grid. Many drivers can live with this limitation most of the time, but few will find the condition satisfactory all of the time. Still, the capabilities that we have today can get us off to a good start.

New technology often shows up in this manner: it is not completely satisfactory in the beginning, but good enough to get going. The first personal computers, for example, were little more than toys. They fascinated cognoscenti [people who have superior knowledge or taste] and hobbyists, but compared to the mainframe computers that were the workhorses of that time, they were limited. PCs quickly grew in capability and eventually reached parity with mainframes and then surpassed them in efficiency and computing power. Such approaches, of starting low and moving up, have been named "disruptive technologies."

The automobile industry, in the main, has not embraced disruptive technology. It has been waiting instead for batteries to improve until they can allow electric cars to enter the marketplace with the same driving range as gasoline-fueled cars. Battery developers, in turn, have been waiting for demand from the automobile industry to develop before fully committing the resources required to do the job. The generation and transmission infrastructures have not been built up to service the potentially explosive demand from transportation. The wait has gone on for some time.

To be sure, this situation is starting to change. Startups like Tesla Motors and Project Better Place have begun to experiment with all-electric cars, and important developments are underway at Nissan and General Motors. But our exposure to the vagaries of oil supply is growing by the month.

We must accelerate conversion to electricity in a major way.

Dual Fuels

To start with, the U.S. government should lead the way by requiring that a growing percentage of new cars be built with *dual-fuel* capability. These dual-fuel cars would have both an electric engine and an auxiliary gasoline engine to augment it. The car would run on electricity, and after the batteries were depleted, it would switch to running on the gasoline engine.

Such dual capabilities are often built into machines to help with technology transitions. When DVD players first came to market, they were often combined with a VCR tape player so the consumer could choose if he wanted to watch a movie in VCR or DVD form. Eventually the DVD player became the default standard, but only after a period of time that allowed consumers and the broader market time to adapt.

Laptop computers today come with both wireless and wired Internet connections. If you are in a hotel, you can choose to use wireless service or plug in to the hotel's wired connection. I expect wireless connectivity eventually will be sufficiently powerful and accessible to obviate the wired alternative.

The same would happen to cars. The forces of disruptive technology would eventually bring about improvements in battery technology, ultimately allowing the production of an all-electric car with satisfactory driving range.

This process, however, won't happen quickly enough on its own. No matter how fast the production of dual-fuel cars is ramped, replacing the bulk of the approximately 250 million cars on the roads in the United States with new cars will take a decade or more. As with PCs, the work of advocates and hobbyists shows the way out of this dilemma. There are enterprising folks who have experimented with converting existing gasoline cars into electric cars by removing the gasoline engine and replacing it with an electric engine. Some are working to devise ways in which existing gasoline cars would be converted to dual-fuel cars. As with the new dual-fuel cars, these cars would give first priority to the electric power stored on board, and switch to gasoline only after the electric power is exhausted.

Shifting to electricity has the added advantage of helping to mitigate a major environmental threat.

Not all vehicles have the space and design that allow this process to happen easily. Luckily, it is the most gasoline-hungry cars that do. Pickups, SUVs, vans, and the like represent about 80 million vehicles, with mileage of perhaps 13 to 16 miles per gallon. Converting these should be our first priority. The instincts of conservationists have been to improve what is already pretty good—compact cars with decent fuel efficiency. Our national priority to decrease the amount of oil-based energy dictates that we go after the low-mileage part of the fleet first.

Estimates show that converting these vehicles to dual-fuel operation, even with electricity providing no more than 50 miles of driving range between daily recharging, could cut petroleum imports by 50 to 60 percent—a stunning opportunity.

The Need for Original Thinking

A task of this magnitude requires major effort and investment. We may need to apply tax incentives to offset the cost of the retrofit and couple them with deep discounts on the cost of electricity used by the vehicle over some initial period, such as one to two years.

Shifting to electricity has the added advantage of helping to mitigate a major environmental threat. A shift from petroleum-based vehicles to electricity-based ones would move the locus for addressing carbon emissions from millions of individual vehicles to far fewer centralized electricity-generating plants. Controlling emissions thus becomes an industrial task, easier technologically. Estimates indicate a potential reduction of carbon emissions of around 50 percent through such a shift.

Are government mandates and incentives really necessary to drive these processes? Can't we rely on market forces?

Automobile manufacturing, battery production, and the generation and transmission of electricity are all represented by different industries—each with its own financial aims. The absence of common interests is a major obstacle to action, requiring the coordinated commitment of several industries.

In his seminal study, the business historian Alfred Chandler found that the growth of new industries is often limited unless appropriate adjustments in their structure take place and the boundaries are redrawn to remove obstacles to growth. Chandler also recognized that the necessary changes are unlikely to happen if we have to count on the incumbent managers to bring them about.

Of course, startups and new ventures, not limited by the economic rules of established industries, can break the gridlock in time. But we don't have the time.

There Could Be Blood

Oil-producing countries flex their muscles more and more openly. The elections in Ukraine led Russia to threaten to cut off natural gas supplies. The need to secure oil seems to have influenced China's attitude toward the genocide in Darfur. In Venezuela, [President] Hugo Chávez is using oil to gain political influence in the hemisphere. "The politics of energy is warping diplomacy in certain parts of the world," said Secretary of State Condoleezza Rice in recent Senate testimony.

And it could get worse. Scratch the surface, and you find that oil has been a major factor in many wars. And it could be again. Today's relationship between China and the United States, says Henry Kissinger, "is very similar to that of Germany, a rising country at the turn of the 20th century, and Britain, an established one." Their conflict over resources "eventually led to war." Listen to Lieutenant General William Caldwell, who heads the Army's schools and training centers: "We are in a period of time in the world today where there is a shortage of resources." Because of this, over the next 10 to 15 years, Army Chief of Staff General George W. Casey Jr. says we will face "an era of persisting conflict."

We have an urgent need for a strategy that can deflect our march toward this "persisting conflict" by strengthening our energy resilience. A policy that favors sticky energy with multiple sources and that aggressively moves vehicles first toward dual-fuel mode and ultimately to running on just electricity provides the answer.

8

Domestic Oil Resources Will Reduce Foreign Dependence

Gary Jason

Gary Jason is a philosopher and the author of Dangerous Thoughts.

Despite the rhetoric by President Obama and others about US reliance on oil imports, domestic oil resources are currently making a comeback. As the cost of oil has risen, it has become profitable to re-open older wells along with developing new sources with advanced technology. In the near future, the US will be able to cut its foreign oil consumption by as much as 60%. While the environmental left continues to promote the idea of green energy, the results have been unpromising. The US should stop throwing away money on projects that attempt to develop alternative sources of energy. The US, thanks to technology innovation and new oil fields, has enough oil to meet its future energy needs.

A rush of recent reports on energy has much to say about the fundamental foolishness of the green vision of energy production, the vision long regnant in academia, and the one that informs the Obama regime.

The green vision—really, the green dream or delusion—is that the world is running out of fossil fuels, and we need to switch to so-called renewable or sustainable sources, such as solar power, wind power, and biofuels. (These "renewable," allegedly low-pollution green options never include nuclear or hydroelectric power, both of which are proven to be cost-effective and clean—a point to which I will return shortly). If we just embrace these "new" energy sources, the greens aver, jobs will just multiply magically. But if we continue to use fossil fuels, we are doomed to economic stagnation.

New Sources for Oil in the US

The first report is the happy news that the number of new American oil wells is increasing at a pace not seen in over three decades.

According to the major oil drilling company Baker Hughes, it installed over 800 new oil rigs last year, over twice the previous year's (2009) total, and a tenfold increase over the yearly average during the late 1990s.

These rigs are placed to tap so-called "unconventional reservoirs," squeezed into shale rock strata. Ten years ago these shale oil reservoirs were written off, but the increase in oil prices and in the level of oil-drilling technology have now opened them up.

By 2020, shale oil fields could allow us to cut our imports of foreign oil by 60%.

The story mentions several promising shale oil fields, including the Eagle Ford formation (stretching from southern Texas into northern Mexico), the Bakken formation (in North Dakota), and the Monterey formation (in California). These formations currently produce about half a million barrels a day. It is now projected that production will hit 1.5 million barrels per day in four years, the equivalent of what we currently get from the Gulf of Mexico, which is roughly about 30% of current total domestic oil production. This will go far toward making up for declining production from our conventional fields in Alaska and the Gulf of Mexico.

The Bakken formation is yielding oil faster than can be sent through pipelines to market, so the oil companies are shipping it by road and rail. The companies have had to open camps to house all the workers needed, and North Dakota has unemployment at less than half the national average (its rate is 3.8%, to be exact). As another article notes, the Bakken field produced 113 million barrels in 2010, up from 33 million the year before.

If the Bakken and Eagle Ford oil fields pay out as expected (they are projected to yield an eventual four billion barrels of oil), they will wind up as the fifth- and sixth- biggest US fields ever found. By 2020, shale oil fields could allow us to cut our imports of foreign oil by 60%, which (at $90 a barrel) is $175 billion less we give foreign dictators. And another article reports that the EIA [Energy Information Administration] estimates that with these new fields, American petroleum production will increase 14% by 2020.

Technological Innovations

A more recent news item gives us more detail about the new shale oil drilling technology. It involves drilling down and then horizontally into the rock, then pumping a mixture of sand, water, and small amount of chemicals in to crack the rock and loosen the oil molecules. Drillers figured out how to make the shale crack more extensively, and that made the extracted oil cheaper than had ever been thought possible.

This process, called fracking, has proven very effective in freeing natural gas. . . . It is beginning to pay off big time in oil production as well.

With this method, new fields are being opened, such as the Leonard formation (which straddles New Mexico and Texas), and the Niobrara formation (which underlies Wyoming, Colorado, Nebraska, and Kansas).

Now, last year, as shale oil technology started proving itself a tremendously effective method for extracting oil, environmentalists immediately arose in opposition. Rep. Henry Waxman (D-CA) held hearings investigating fracking, and the environmentalist Left produced a documentary (*Gasland*) alleging that the technology was poisoning groundwater. But all the EPA [Environmental Protection Agency] studies have shown that fracking is safe, and even the Environmental Defense Fund seems comfortable with it.

The Myth of Green Energy

So much for the death of petroleum. Turning now to renewable-green energy sources, some interesting stories are worth noting. Let's begin with the report that France's solar program is in trouble.

Two years ago, the French National Assembly passed a law requiring France's national utility, Electricité de France (EDF), to buy all the power produced by newly installed solar panels at $745 per megawatt-hour, roughly ten times the market price for electricity. The goal was to increase the number of people installing solar panels on their roofs.

The Chinese-manufactured solar panels have a large "carbon footprint"—meaning they were produced by using large amounts of power generated by the burning of dirty coal.

The intended result was that applications for rooftop panel array connections rose—from 7,000 applications *a year* before the subsidiary to about 3,000 *a day* by December of last year. But there were unintended, though embarrassingly foreseeable, consequences. One was that the cost to EDF of buying solar power has exploded to $1.4 billion a year, and is threatening its financial health. EDF saw its stock drop by 20% in 2010 (compare that to a 3.7% drop for Europe's Stoxx 600 Utilities Index). EDF is now $78 billion in debt, a situation that has caused it to defer modernizing its 53 nuclear reactors (which provide 75% of France's electricity). And it has had to jack up the surcharge that consumers who don't use solar panels have to pay.

A second consequence is that the solar panels are being purchased from China, thus shifting jobs from France to there. Worse, the Chinese solar panels have a large "carbon footprint"—meaning they were produced by using large amounts of power generated by the burning of dirty coal!

Failed Domestic Energy Projects

Then there is the report about an ethanol plant, Range Fuels, that in 2007 received startup subsidies of $76 million from the federal government and $6 million from the lucky state of Georgia, where it was supposed to open a plant making ethanol from pine chips. The next year, it got a loan for $80 million, guaranteed by taxpayers under the "Biorefinery Assistance Program."

The reason the [President George W.] Bush administration started pushing this "advanced biofuels cellulosic ethanol" program (essentially, a program for producing ethanol from switch grass and other biomass) was that corn-based ethanol was already rapidly acquiring a bad reputation for excessive costs and a low yield of energy outputs. Cellulosic ethanol looked like a better prospect.

Georgia politicians were so excited by the smell of pork [government funding that benefits a specific group or locale] that they started calling their state "the Saudi Arabia of Pine Trees." *The Saudi Arabia of pine trees!*

Well, guess what? Range Fuels just closed, having never produced even one shot of ethanol. Gone with the wind, as they used to say in Atlanta. And all the subsidy money gone with it.

Honest to God, you couldn't make this stuff up.

9

Military Expenditures Drastically Increase the True Cost of Foreign Oil

Peter Maass

Peter Maass is a contributing writer to the New York Times Magazine *and author of* Crude World.

While most people believe the cost of oil can be measured at the pump, the true cost of fuel has long been hidden. The biggest hidden addition involves military spending: most military actions take place in oil rich countries in the Middle East to protect resources important to the United States. Unfortunately, this is an issue that almost no politician wishes to discuss. As American oil consumption continues to increase following the British Petroleum spill and the Iraq War, it has been left up to experts outside of the government to highlight the true cost of imported oil.

Shortly after the Marines rolled into Baghdad and tore down a statue of Saddam Hussein, I visited the Ministry of Oil. American troops surrounded the sand-colored building, protecting it like a strategic jewel. But not far away, looters were relieving the National Museum of its actual jewels. Baghdad had become a carnival of looting. A few dozen Iraqis who worked at the Oil Ministry were gathered outside the American cordon, and one of them, noting the protection afforded his workplace and the lack of protection everywhere else, remarked to me, "It is all about oil."

The issue he raised is central to figuring out what we truly pay for a gallon of gas. The BP [British Petroleum] spill in the Gulf of Mexico has reminded Americans that the price at the pump is only a down payment; an honest calculation must include the contamination of our waters, land, and air. Yet the calculation remains incomplete if we don't consider other factors too, especially what might be the largest externalized cost of all: the military one. To what extent is oil linked to the wars we fight and the more than half-trillion dollars we spend on our military every year? We are in an era of massive deficits, so it pays to know what we are paying for and how much it costs.

This is one of the tricky things about oil, the hidden costs, and one of the reasons we are addicted to the substance—we don't acknowledge its full price.

The True Cost of Oil

The debate often hovers at a sandbox level of did-so/did-not. Donald Rumsfeld, the former defense secretary, insisted the invasion of Iraq had "nothing to do with oil." But even Alan Greenspan, the former Federal Reserve chairman, rejected that line. "It is politically inconvenient to acknowledge what everyone knows," Greenspan wrote in his memoir. "The Iraq war is largely about oil." If it is even *partly* true that we invade for oil and maintain a navy and army for oil, how much is that costing? This is one of the tricky things about oil, the hidden costs, and one of the reasons we are addicted to the substance—we don't acknowledge its full price.

If we wish to know, we can. An innovative approach comes from Roger Stern, an economic geographer at Princeton University who in April published a peer-reviewed study on the cost of keeping aircraft carriers in the Persian Gulf from 1976 to 2007. Because carriers patrol the gulf for the explicit mission of securing oil shipments, Stern was on solid ground in attributing that cost to oil. He had found an excellent metric. He combed through the Defense Department's data—which is not easy to do because the Pentagon does not disaggregate its expenditures by region or mission—and came up with a total, over three decades, of $7.3 trillion. Yes, *trillion*.

And that's just a partial accounting of peacetime spending. It's far trickier to figure out the extent to which America's wars are linked to oil and then put a price tag on it. But let's assume that Rumsfeld, in an off-the-record moment of retirement candor, might be persuaded to acknowledge that the invasion of Iraq was *somewhat* related to oil. A 2008 study by Nobel Prize-winner Joseph Stiglitz and Harvard University budget expert Linda Bilmes put the cost of that war—everything spent up to that point and likely to be spent in the years ahead—at a minimum of $3 trillion (and probably much more). Again, *trillion*.

Of course we would have to wait a long time before finding a PowerPoint presentation in the Pentagon or White House (no matter the party in power) on defense spending for oil. Just as cuts to Social Security are a third rail [a sensitive political issue], an accounting of oil-related military spending is nearly unheard of in the halls of power. For politicians and generals, it is a slippery slope: Speak too loudly on the subject, and they risk undercutting the we-only-want-to-make-the-world-a-better-place notion of U.S. foreign policy. It's easier to let the debate idle at vague rhetoric rather than hard numbers.

Out-of-Government Experts

You would have to go back nearly 20 years to get anything on the subject from the Government Accountability Office (GAO), the investigative arm of the U.S. government that in

1991 estimated that between 1980 and 1990 the United States spent a total of $366 billion to defend oil supplies in the Middle East. The GAO report was just a snapshot of one region in a limited time frame a long time ago when America was not fighting a major war there or elsewhere. The study would have been a good start if it had been followed by other studies that went deeper and further, but that didn't happen.

The United States consumes more gasoline today than on the day Iraq was invaded and the day of the BP accident.

So it has fallen to a cottage industry of out-of-government experts like Stiglitz and Stern to examine metrics that measure oil's connections to not just war but corruption and poverty. These experts include Paul Collier of Oxford University, who wrote *The Bottom Billion*, as well as Michael Ross at UCLA, Michael Watts at UC Berkeley, Ian Gary at Oxfam, and Sarah Wykes, formerly with the NGO Global Witness. Their areas of expertise—economics, geography, political science, corruption—as well as the metrics on which they focus, are similar to the unconventional backgrounds and ideas of the experts whom Gen. David Petraeus called on to rethink the metrics and practice of counterinsurgency.

Oil has yet to find its Petraeus; it remains a badly quantified problem. The abstraction of global warming, the pity of oil-soaked pelicans, even battlefield deaths in Iraq—these have not occasioned real changes in our addiction to all things petroleum. The United States consumes more gasoline today than on the day Iraq was invaded and the day of the BP accident. If I had a dollar for every time a politician said, as President Barack Obama did in his Oval Office energy speech in June, "The time to embrace a clean energy future is now," I could build a wind farm. An honest accounting would do a lot more than tired platitudes because it would force us to confront the hidden costs that we don't see at the pump. And after all, the best way to get the attention of consumers is through their pocketbooks.

10

Oil Companies Should Bear the True Costs of Oil

Mark Engler

Mark Engler is a senior analyst with Foreign Policy in Focus.

Even in the wake of oil spills in Alaska and the Gulf of Mexico, companies like British Petroleum and Exxon continue to make record profits. In fact, these companies—despite lawsuits and fines—never completely pay for the damage these disasters cause. Part of the reason these companies remain so profitable, then, is because there is never a true accounting of the cost of oil. The cost of gas at the pump, for instance, does not take into account public monies spent to curb environmental problems caused by oil spills. Likewise, the cost of gas never includes the subsidies that many oil companies receive at taxpayer expense. America's dependence on oil will remain problematic until corporations like Exxon and BP are properly regulated and forced to pay the true costs of oil.

This might be an opportune time to make a disclosure: I am a BP [British Petroleum] shareholder. Admittedly, I've never attended the company's annual meeting, and if I did, I would have very little weight to throw around.

I own two shares of BP stock. I received my stake in the company as a Christmas gift in 1989, when I was 14 years old. The previous June, I had taken a "summer enrichment" course in the Des Moines public schools, designed as an introduction to the world of business. The teacher gave each of us in the class a modest hypothetical budget to invest in the stock market.

Earnest young capitalists, we made our picks and then followed the quotes in the morning paper. I invested heavily in Amoco and finished the summer feeling that my portfolio had done quite well. As a result, my younger brother decided that I should receive a real piece of the enterprise that was once John D. Rockefeller's Standard Oil. He conspired with my mom to get me an Amoco share for the holidays.

Oil Profits

I've watched the oil industry as an interested party ever since. In 1998, my Amoco stock split, turning my one share into two. Then, a few months later, the company was acquired by BP. This "oil mega-merger," as the BBC [British Broadcasting Corporation] called it, gave me a stake in yet another energy titan. It also allowed the combined corporation to shed 6,000 jobs, prompting its new chief executive, Sir John Browne of BP, to confidently assure the press that "he hoped the merger will increase pre-tax profits of the two partners by 'at least' two billion dollars by the end of 2000."

It's time for a different accounting.

The merger proved profitable indeed. Over time, the price of my stock nearly doubled. I received dividends every three months, usually of around 60 cents per share. And by the mid-2000s, BP was making some $20 billion per year in profits. The numbers looked good.

Of course, these are not the only numbers to consider. In fact, in the wake of BP's disaster in the Gulf of Mexico, they don't seem like the right numbers at all. It's time for a different accounting: What has that catastrophic spill cost our society? What price do we pay for our dependence on oil? How do we measure these things?

Costs of Business

When I first began receiving Amoco's annual reports, they featured photos that celebrated robust industrial capabilities, like multicolored sunsets behind fields of horsehead oil pumps in Texas. These days, there's still some of that, but the reports tend to have more shots of solar panels, white windmills, and smiling school children (our future). Someone looking at the annual review the company sent me in 2001, for instance, might have been fooled by the photos of lush, palm-heavy landscapes in Indonesia, California, and Trinidad into thinking that it was a mailing from Conservation International.

Such changes in public relations were born of tragedy. Back in 1989, not three months before my summer business class, the Exxon Valdez collided with the Bligh reef in Alaska's Prince William Sound, breaching its hull. Even according to conservative estimates, it spilled more than 10 million gallons of oil and contaminated more than 1,200 miles of ecologically sensitive coastline. For years afterwards, we saw Exxon deal with the fallout of the catastrophe.

However many thousands of boats and booms the company deployed, it only managed to recover about 8% of the oil released. The rest evaporated, coated beaches, or sank to the bottom of the sea. The Exxon Valdez Oil Spill Trustee Council estimates that 250,000 seabirds, 2,800 sea otters, 300 harbor seals, 250 bald eagles, up to 22 killer whales, and billions of salmon and herring eggs were killed by the spill. Two decades later, some 16,000 gallons of leftover oil still poison wildlife in the Prince William Sound.

Lawsuits and Fines

The cost to the planet was steep. The cost to Exxon could have been severe as well. While the company claims that it spent $2.1 billion on its clean-up efforts, it might have had to pay many times that in fines and lawsuit settlements. The government initially threatened $5 billion in criminal penalties, and in 1994 a federal jury ordered the company to pay $5.2 billion in punitive damages to Alaskans who had filed a class-action lawsuit. For a time, things at Exxon looked grim.

Although these were the worries of a rival corporation, Amoco investors did get a taste of what Exxon was experiencing. In 1990, after a dozen years of litigation, a federal judge in Chicago ordered my company to pay $132 million in damages to the French government and other parties. They had all been harmed 12 years earlier when the Amoco Cadiz ran aground off the coast of Brittany, releasing 68 million gallons of oil. At the time, it was the largest tanker spill ever. It killed millions of sea urchins and mollusks, thousands of tons of oysters, and almost 20,000 birds.

In terms of the overall business, however, the judgment was only a blip on Amoco's radar screen. In the end, Exxon never made any $10 billion payout for its disaster either. The first Bush administration allowed the company to plead guilty to a small number of charges and settled for penalties and fines of around $1 billion. The judge who ultimately approved the settlement had earlier worried that the amount was too low: "I'm afraid these fines send the wrong message," he said, "and suggest that spills are a cost of business that can be absorbed."

It was a prescient concern, especially given the resolution of the class-action suit. In that arena, Exxon's lawyers proved patient and skilled. They held up the case in court for years until, in 2008, nearly two decades after the spill, the Supreme Court ruled that damages paid by the company would be limited to an exceptionally absorbable $507.5 million.

Emerging Unscathed

In the months during which the well under BP's Deepwater Horizon freely spewed crude into the Gulf of Mexico, it released 4.9 million barrels of oil, or 205.8 million gallons, according to a government panel tasked with measuring the spill. Depending on what estimates you use for the earlier disaster, this amounts to roughly 20 times as much oil as the Exxon Valdez released. In negotiations with the Obama administration, BP agreed to put $20 billion into a fund for cleanup. It has also indicated that it will pay "all legitimate claims" related to the disaster.

A price tag of $167 per seagull seems tragically inadequate as a means of accounting for a destroyed population of birds.

Despite such vows, how much of the final cost BP will actually end up paying is unclear. Spill-related damages and lost economic activity could amount to tens of billions of dollars more than what BP is currently setting aside. An Oxford Economics study predicts that costs to the tourism industry alone could exceed $22 billion. Damage to the natural environment, much of it potentially unseen, is almost impossible to quantify.

In the case of the Valdez spill, according to the Associated Press, "the state priced each seagull at $167, eagles at $22,000, harbor seals at $700, and killer whales at $300,000." Such an effort could be replicated for the Gulf. Yet a price tag of $167 per seagull seems tragically inadequate as a means of accounting for a destroyed population of birds, and it doesn't begin to account for species that may seem less significant to us, but could be crucial to the ecosystem.

Now-deposed BP executive Tony Hayward repeatedly vowed to Gulf residents that the company would "make this right." Likewise, in 1989, after the Valdez ran aground, Don Cornett, Exxon's top official in Alaska, told locals dependent on the ruined fishing industry, "We will do whatever it takes to keep you whole. We do business straight." Of course, that was before Exxon went on to pursue years of dogged litigation to limit its liability.

Once the public furor dies down, as already seems to be happening, BP will have financial incentive to do the same. Though the price of my stock took a hit, plummeting from around $60 per share in early April—before anyone had heard of the Deepwater Horizon—to a low of $27 per share in late June, it has already rallied to above $40 as of this writing. Some analysts are betting that BP, like Exxon, will contain the cost of its spill, and then continue about its business in much the same manner it did before. As analyst Antonia Juhasz argues with regard to the Valdez disaster, "Exxon emerged virtually unscathed from the incident and is, today, the most profitable corporation the world has ever known." . . .

Gushing Subsidies

Military spending is just one type of public subsidy that benefits the oil industry and keeps the price at gas stations artificially low. When I made my adolescent wager on Amoco, I was not aware that the company also profited from massive tax breaks and other non-military forms of support. Yet these go a long way toward making the enterprise a safe bet for investors. . . .

Some analysts are betting that BP, like Exxon, will contain the cost of its spill, and then continue about its business in much the same manner it did before.

In early July, *The New York Times* reported: "With federal officials now considering a new tax on petroleum production to pay for [the BP oil spill] cleanup, the industry is fighting the measure. . . But an examination of the American tax code indicates that oil production is among the most heavily subsidized businesses, with tax breaks available at virtually every stage of the exploration and extraction process." Senator Robert Menendez (D-NJ) added, "The flow of revenues to oil companies is like the gusher at the bottom of the Gulf of Mexico: heavy and constant. There is no reason for these corporations to shortchange the American taxpayer."

Government ... maintains a massive highway system that facilitates gas-intensive auto travel, only part of which is paid for by taxes on motorists.

The *Times* story notes that BP was, for instance, able to write off 70% of what it was paying in rent for the Deepwater Horizon rig that caught fire, "a deduction of more than $225,000 a day since the lease began." Amazingly, BP is also claiming a $9.9 billion tax credit for its response to its oil spill in the Gulf of Mexico.

Not only does our government allow energy companies to avoid taxes in myriad ways, the variety of public supports for the oil industry outside the tax code are almost too numerous to list. A 1995 report by the Union of Concerned Scientists mentioned several, including these: the government invests in substantial energy research that directly benefits the oil industry; it spends millions to maintain a Strategic Petroleum Reserve, designed to help stabilize the oil supply; and it maintains a massive highway system that facilitates gas-intensive auto travel, only part of which is paid for by taxes on motorists.

The Environmental Cost of Oil

Then, of course, there is the environmental price we pay, most notably in the form of global warming. As Ezra Klein wrote recently in *Newsweek*, some experts argue that carbon emissions from cars could be offset at the cost of about 65 cents per gallon (money that would presumably be invested in activities like reforestation). Others believe the cost would be much steeper—perhaps steep enough to turn oil industry profits into losses.

Andrew Simms of the British New Economics Foundation calculated that, if you were to combine BP's exploration, extraction, and production activities with those involved in the sale of its products, you would end up with 1,458 million tons of CO_2-equivalent entering the atmosphere per year. Pricing the cost of carbon emissions at $35 per ton, he puts the bill for climate-change damages at $51 billion. Since BP reported a *mere* $19 billion in profits in 2006, the year Simms was reviewing, he argues that it would have been "$31 billion in the red," or effectively bankrupt, if it had to cover the climate-change bill.

There's more, too. Consider that car exhaust and oil industry pollution mean an increase in smog and asthma, burdening our health-care system. Then count in the damage caused by massive oil spills we seldom hear about in places like Nigeria, Ecuador, or China, as well as the economic cost of traffic congestion and excess auto accidents made possible by subsidized car travel (costs which the willfully contrarian *Freakonomics* blog contends may be even more expensive than global warming). The final tally is staggering. High-end estimates of the true costs of the gas we use come to over $15 per gallon. Taxpayers subsidize significant parts of this sum without even knowing it.

That Which Makes Life Worthwhile

To the extent that energy corporations are made to spend more to do business in the future—forced, for example, to pay for mandatory safety measures, pricier insurance policies, or taxes from which they were previously exempt—some of the costs of oil could be "internalized." If enough costs were accounted for, some companies, no longer confident that their efforts would be profitable, might begin to reconsider exploiting harder-to-extract reserves of fossil fuels. A recent article in the British *Guardian* offered this scenario: "If the billions of dollars of annual subsidies and the many tax breaks the industry gets were withdrawn, and the cost of protecting oil companies in developing countries were added, then most of the world's oil would almost certainly be left in the ground."

Unfortunately, this is surely an overstatement. If the exploits of oil companies were made more costly, these companies would simply raise their prices and pass along the costs to consumers. And we would pay them because we are unwilling to give up the speed and convenience of driving, or the luxury of airline travel. We would pay them because we are unwilling to reduce our consumption of foods shipped to our grocery stores from far away, or diminish our energy consumption in many other ways. We would pay them in order to maintain at least a facsimile of our previous lives.

Or would we?

While it is too much to say that "most of the world's oil" would be abandoned, some might be. In 2008, when gas prices soared above $4 per gallon, Americans did behave differently. As the *New York Times* reported, we drove 10 billion fewer miles per month than the year before; surprising numbers of SUV owners traded in their vehicles for smaller, more efficient cars; and daily oil consumption was lowered by 900,000 barrels. Investors began to reconsider how "realistic" the costs of developing alternative energies might be and to fund them more seriously. In other words, Americans responded to the market.

This was a hopeful sign. At the same time, reacting to the market's cues will not be enough to sort out our relationship to oil and the oil business. We must also reckon with the market's limits. Appreciating the full magnitude of the Deepwater Horizon crisis requires us to recognize that the market is inherently unable to account for many of the things we hold most precious. Robert F. Kennedy pointed to this problem in one of his most powerful speeches, explaining that the gross national product measures everything "except that which makes life worthwhile."

Beyond Spreadsheets

Some things cannot be—or should not be—left to business spreadsheets. Calculating the cost of a destroyed ecosystem in the Gulf of Mexico or along the coast of Alaska means putting a price tag on things that are not meant to be priced. If you accept that a harbor seal's life is indeed worth $700, and a killer whale's $300,000, pretty soon you must accept that your own life has a price tag on it as well.

Yet taking the limits of economic calculus seriously has implications. It means that we cannot trust the market to solve its own problems—to self-regulate and self-correct. It means that we need democratic action to place controls on corporate behavior. It means that some things must be considered not merely expensive but sacred, and defended against forces blind to their true value.

Those who believe that the price of my BP stock will recover in the next year might be wrong. Even if the stock bottoms out, however, that won't restore a shattered Gulf, nor will it change a system that prizes easy consumption and deferred responsibility. We can only correct for the catastrophe oil has wrought by living according to a different measure.

11

Methanol Can Reduce Foreign Oil Dependence

Robert Zubrin

Robert Zubrin is the president of Pioneer Astronautics and author of Energy Victory.

The US will never achieve energy independence as long as it relies on oil imports. Fortunately, there is another fuel available, methanol, and it has several advantages over oil. Methanol can be processed from multiple resources, is cheaper to make than gasoline, and has environmental benefits because it burns clean. Also, most cars can easily be converted to methanol use. The only thing standing in the way of the methanol solution is the need for government action to deregulate the industry.

The United States currently produces 8 percent of the world's liquid fuel but uses 25 percent, making up the difference by importing 5 billion barrels of oil annually. With prices currently near $100 per barrel, this dependency will cost us $500 billion this year, an amount equal to the nation's entire trade deficit. Furthermore, at a time when Congress is seeking to keep taxes light in order to boost job creation, our dependency will impose a tax on our economy equal to 20 percent of what Americans pay the IRS [Internal Revenue Service]. Except, of course, that these revenues will go to the treasuries of foreign governments instead of our own.

During the 1940s, the United States produced 60 percent of the world's liquid fuel. This advantage proved to be a major factor in securing the Allied victory in World War II. Had we been as weak in energy security then as we are today, we might well have lost the war, as enemy submarines could have collapsed our economy, and with it our war effort, simply by cutting off our oil supply.

If we are to break free of the crushing economic burden and national-security threat that oil dependency imposes, we need to triple our liquid-fuel production. There is no realistic way that this can be done through expanding domestic drilling for oil, multiplying the yield of corn ethanol (which now accounts for 20 percent of domestic liquid-fuel production), or a combination of the two. Rather, we need a new source of liquid fuel, one that can be produced easily and economically, from resources available to us, and on the vast scale required to address the deficiency.

The resources available to support expanded methanol production are vast.

Replacing Oil with Methanol

Fortunately, such a fuel is available. It is methanol, also known as wood alcohol. In contrast to algae oils and cellulosic ethanol, methanol is not a futuristic pipe dream touted by researchers seeking funding. Rather, it is one of the world's top five chemical commodities, with an operating global annual production capacity of 27 billion gallons, and a current spot price, without any subsidies, of $1.28 per gallon. While methanol contains only about half the energy per gallon of gasoline, its excellent octane rating of 105 allows it to be burned more efficiently, making $1.28-per-gallon methanol equivalent to $2-per-gallon gasoline. All in all, a very competitive price.

The resources available to support expanded methanol production are vast. In contrast to gasoline—which can be made economically only from petroleum—or ethanol—whose mass production requires the use of sugars or starches— methanol can readily be made from any carbon-containing material. To list a few of methanol's potential sources: oil, natural gas, coal, urban garbage, or any kind of biomass without exception.

The United States possesses around 4 billion metric tons (29.5 billion barrels) of proven oil reserves. This would barely be enough to support a fully fuel-independent America for four years. In contrast, our proven coal reserves exceed 270 billion tons, and our natural-gas reserves may be nearly as great. North America currently produces about 40 billion metric tons per year of biomass, of which 2 billion tons are harvested as farm and forestry products and 1 billion tons discarded as agricultural and forestry waste. We also discard approximately a quarter-billion tons per year of carbonaceous urban trash. Thus, taken together, our resources for methanol production not only are up to fully replacing our current oil imports, but are up to supporting the growing demands of an expanding economy for decades or centuries to come.

Methanol burns cleaner than gasoline, causing much less particulate pollution. It is also safer—it is much less likely to catch fire in the event of a crash, and its fumes contain none of gasoline's rich mixture of carcinogens. While, unlike ethanol, methanol is not edible, it is not especially toxic. In fact, windshield-wiper fluid is one-third methanol, and, because it is readily biodegradable, it has been handled by the public and released onto roads worldwide in vast quantities for decades without any impact on public health or the environment.

Cars and Methanol

If we could convert our auto fleet to run on methanol, the $500 billion per year we are now paying foreign potentates for oil could go instead to American businesses and workers to produce our fuel right here at home. On average, it takes $100,000 of GDP [gross domestic product] to create one job. At that rate, the $500 billion spent here instead of abroad would create 5 million American jobs directly, and millions more indirectly from the construction, retail, and service industries that would be supported by the methanol workers' paychecks. This would help address our critical national and state deficits as well, as millions of people would go from the unemployment rolls to the tax rolls.

But can we readily open our vehicle-fuel market to methanol? The simple answer is yes, and quickly. The large majority of cars sold in the U.S. today (and for at least the last five years), including all GM and Ford vehicles, have been equipped with computers and chromated fuel lines that make them potentially capable of flex-fuel operation. If provided with the right software, and with methanol-impervious Buna-N rubber seals (costing less than 50 cents per vehicle) for their fuel system, every new car sold in the U.S. could be fully flex-fuel, capable of running equally well on methanol, ethanol, or gasoline.

We can break our fatal dependence on foreign oil, but Congress needs to act.

There is currently a bill before Congress—the Open Fuel Standard bill (HR-1687), co-sponsored by a bipartisan group including Reps. John Shimkus (R., Ill.) and Eliot Engel (D., N.Y.)—that would require flex-fuel capability of the majority of new cars sold in America. If the bill passes, a market for methanol would be created that would very quickly call into being expanded production and distribution facilities, both in the U.S. and elsewhere. This would force gasoline into competition with methanol at the pump worldwide, thereby putting in place a permanent global competitive constraint on the price of oil. Thus owners of older cars, which are incapable of methanol operation, would also benefit, since their gasoline would be cheaper. And once methanol pumps become widely available, many drivers would see the benefit of spending a few hundred dollars to have their seals replaced and cars re-programmed to obtain fuel choice. The switch to a predominantly methanol-fueled vehicle fleet could thus take place very rapidly.

The Open Fuel Standard bill would unchain the Invisible Hand, creating a true free market in vehicle fuels. Those reluctant to embrace it need to answer the following question: In whose interest is it that Americans should continue to be denied fuel choice?

We can break our fatal dependence on foreign oil, but Congress needs to act.

12

Public Transportation Can Reduce Foreign Oil Dependence

Robert J. Shapiro, Kevin A. Hassett, and Frank S. Arnold

Robert J. Shapiro is the managing director of Sonecon; Kevin A. Hassett is a resident scholar of the American Enterprise Institute; and Frank S. Arnold is the president of Applied Microeconomics, Inc.

Public transportation has the potential to help with a number of problems associated with importing oil. Public transportation is more efficient than using automobiles, leading to cleaner air and less energy consumption. Public transportation also saves money because fewer highways need to be constructed and maintained. Increasing public transportation use in the United States is an achievable goal.

At its current levels of use, public transportation is reducing Americans' energy bills.

- For every passenger mile traveled, public transportation is twice as fuel efficient as private automobiles.

- Per year, public transportation saves more than 855 million gallons of gasoline, or 45 million barrels of oil. This is equal to about one month of oil imports from Saudi Arabia; three months of the energy that Americans use to heat, cool and operate their homes; or half the energy used to manufacture all computers and electronic equipment in America.

Better air quality

Even at current rates of use, public transportation greatly improves air quality. Compared to private vehicles:

- Public transportation produces 95% less carbon monoxide (CO), more than 92% fewer volatile organic compounds (VOCs) and nearly half as much carbon dioxide (CO_2) and nitrogen oxides (NOx)—for every passenger mile traveled.

- Public transportation reduces annual emissions of the pollutants that create smog—VOCs and NOx—by more than 70,000 tons and 27,000 tons respectively.

These reductions equal:

- nearly 50% of all VOCs emitted from the dry cleaning industry, a major source of this pollutant

- 45% of VOCs emitted from the industrial uses of coal

- 50% of NOx from the industrial uses of coal

- more than 33% of the NOx emitted by all domestic oil and gas producers or by the metal processing industry

---

Public transportation reduces emissions of CO_2 . . . by more than 7.4 million tons a year.

In addition, the reduced VOC and NOx emissions that result from public transportation use save between $130 million and $200 million a year in regulatory costs.

Other emissions reduced

- Public transportation reduces CO emissions by nearly 745,000 tons annually. This equals nearly 75% of the CO emissions by all U.S. chemical manufacturers.

- Public transportation reduces emissions of CO_2, which contributes to global warming, by more than 7.4 million tons a year.

The Most Effective Strategy

Americans use more energy for transportation than for any other activity. Nearly 43% of America's energy resources are used in transportation, compared to industrial use (39%), residential use (11%) and commercial use (7%). Greater use of public transportation therefore offers the single most effective strategy currently available for achieving significant energy savings and improving air quality, without imposing new taxes, government mandates or regulations.

Public transportation in Europe

If Americans used public transportation at the same rate as Europeans—for roughly 10% of their daily travel needs—the U.S. would:

- Reduce its dependence on imported oil by more than 40%, or nearly the amount of oil we import from Saudi Arabia each year

- Save more energy every year than all the energy used by the U.S. petrochemical industry and nearly equal the energy used to produce food in the U.S.

- Reduce CO_2 emissions by more than 25% of the Kyoto Agreement [a mandate limiting CO_2 emissions] mandate

- Reduce CO pollution by three times the combined levels emitted by the four highest-polluting industries (chemical manufacturing, oil and gas production, metals processing, and industrial use of coal)

- Reduce smog across the country by cutting NOx emissions by 35% of the combined NOx emissions from the four industries cited above, and cut VOC pollution by 84% of the combined VOC emissions from these four industries

Similar statistics apply to Canada, where public transportation accounts for roughly 7% of that country's daily travel needs.

Modest increases would make a difference

Even modest increases in the uses of public transportation would greatly reduce hazardous pollution in congested areas where pollution now poses the greatest risk.

Achieving a genuine measure of energy independence and cleaner air by investing in our public transportation systems has significant economic advantages.

For example, about half of the 35 largest public transportation systems, serving 26 metropolitan areas, are located in "nonattainment areas" that currently fail to meet EPA [Environmental Protection Agency] air quality standards for CO or smog. In these highly populated urban and suburban areas, the pollution reductions that public transportation can deliver would go directly to improving air quality.

Economic gains

Achieving a genuine measure of energy independence and cleaner air by investing in our public transportation systems has significant economic advantages. While the study measured current and potential benefits of public transportation, the findings suggest that achieving greater energy savings and improvements in air quality by significantly increasing passenger loads on public transportation vehicles would:

- Be less costly than continuing to expand the fleet of private vehicles, and to build and maintain more roads and highways to accommodate them

- Absorb the rising energy, air quality and congestion expenses of this approach

An Achievable Goal for Americans

Increasing use of public transportation is a realistic objective for Americans. In the early 20th century, the U.S. led the world in public transportation development and use, demonstrating that efficient public transportation is a realistic objective in this country. Today, a public transportation renaissance is underway in the U.S. Specifically:

- Since 1995, use of public transportation has grown sharply, and faster than the use of private vehicles.

- Passenger miles accrued on public buses and rail systems have grown faster than the passenger miles accrued in private automobiles, sport utility vehicles and light trucks.

- Public transportation ridership has grown at a faster rate than air travel in recent years.

Making much greater use of public transportation may be the most effective strategy to sharply reduce our dependence on foreign oil and make historic strides in air quality. These results can be achieved if we make public transportation a vital part of our nations energy and air quality policies.

13

The Pickens Plan to Reduce Oil Dependence Is Not Realistic

Vaclav Smil

Vaclav Smil is a professor at the University of Manitoba in Canada.

While there is a great deal to admire about T. Boone Pickens' energy plan, many of his ideas may not be realistic. Whether considering the use of wind power or the conversion of cars to natural gas, these ideas would require state and federal governments to push through new legislation. This would be a difficult task. It also remains unclear whether the plan can be accomplished within the time limits Pickens proposes. One technical challenge, for instance, is the need to have more gas stations that carry natural gas in order for any fuel conversion of cars to be practical. The United States needs a solution to the problem of imported oil. It remains uncertain, however, whether the Pickens Plan is the right solution.

For the past two months, it has been hard to avoid T. Boone Pickens, the 80-year-old Texas oilman, billionaire, and former corporate raider. First, he was all over the TV news introducing his grand, 10-year energy plan for America, which calls for massive construction of wind power turbines and powering many of the country's cars on natural gas. Then he

Vaclav Smil, "A Reality Check on the Pickens Energy Plan," Yale Environment 360 online, August 25, 2008. www.e360.yale.edu.

testified before Congress, warning that the U.S.'s oil addiction—the nation spends $700 billion a year importing oil—amounted to the greatest transfer of wealth in the history of mankind. Soon he was back on TV with a $58 million advertising blitz to rally public support for his proposal, the Pickens Plan.

There is much to admire in the Pickens Plan, but its sheer grandiosity raises serious doubts as to whether it can be realized.

Ever the shrewd entrepreneur—Pickens is building the world's biggest wind farm in Texas and owns the country's largest network of natural gas filling stations—he framed the reasons for taking these radical steps in a concise and accurate manner: America's addiction to oil "threatens our economy, our environment and our national security . . . and it ties our hands as a nation and a people."

There is much to admire in the Pickens Plan, but its sheer grandiosity raises serious doubts as to whether it can be realized: It would require building more than 100,000 wind turbines, connecting them to large cities with at least 40,000 miles of transmission lines, and converting tens of millions of cars to natural gas fuel. To accomplish this within a decade would be a Herculean effort that simply may not be achievable.

The Pickens Plan and Washington Politics

Perhaps the greatest appeal of the Pickens Plan is its cascading simplicity. First, Pickens wants to dot the Great Plains ("the Saudi Arabia of wind power") with wind turbines to replace all the electricity currently produced by burning natural gas. Second, he wants to use the natural gas freed by wind-powered generation to run efficient and clean natural gas vehicles. Third, he believes that this substitution will create a massive, new domestic aerospace-like industry—with well-paying jobs in the production of giant turbines and auxiliary equipment—that will bring economic revival to the depopulating Great Plains. Finally, Pickens says his plan would reduce the huge outflow of wealth to oil-producing nations as the U.S. cuts its oil imports by more than one-third.

If this were an opera, shouts of "Bravissimo!" would be in order. But despite its many positives, the timely realization of the Pickens Plan faces a number of extraordinary challenges, to say the least. The engineering and financial hurdles are daunting: Pickens proposes $1 trillion in private investment to build the wind turbines that will stretch from the Texas panhandle to the Canadian border and another $200 billion (a conservative estimate) to construct a new electric grid connecting this archipelago of wind farms to major cities. Indeed, his plan is so ambitious that he compares it to the construction of the Interstate Highway System in the 1950s.

Alas, that booming era in American history is long gone, and Pickens is proposing his plan in a country where the political system is gridlocked and the economic problems are deep. The realities of today's America—the state of its finances (huge deficits everywhere), the demise of its manufacturing (rising dependence on imports of all kind), and the devaluation of its currency—do not create an impression of a vigorous seeker of new paths; besides, addicts are not usually zealous agents of their own recovery, and addiction to imported oil is exceedingly strong.

So while I would love to see this grand Texan challenge succeed, America's dysfunctional leadership may yet prove its undoing. The plan would require some resolute federal and state legislative decisions. Yet how can we take seriously a Congress which, just two weeks after its members applauded the Pickens Plan, balked at extending the wind energy tax credits essential to the success of the project? Those credits expire at the end of the year. In addition, the plan would have to comply with a multitude of laws and regulations (from environmental assessments to complicated rights-of-way easements), and some of its components would certainly be challenged in the courts, delaying its completion. Pickens apparently appreciates that the plan can be taken seriously only if a well-organized media campaign puts serious political pressure on Congress and helps weaken the many federal and state regulatory obstacles.

An Overly Optimistic Plan

However, unlike Al Gore's utterly unrealistic plan—which calls for entirely "re-powering" America in a decade by completely replacing the enormous fossil-fuel electricity infrastructure with renewable sources—the Pickens Plan sets out a challenging, but not impossible, technical goal. Gore's plan not only assumes an impossibly short timeline, but it also promises totally unrealistic, microchip-like declines in the cost of these new energy sources.

With Pickens' plan, the cost estimates are essentially correct as far as today's prices go. But megaprojects extending over a decade tend to have serious cost overruns, thus Pickens' plan could cost twice as much as is now estimated.

Even more importantly, it is unclear if Pickens appreciates the many technical challenges that have to be solved to make the plan work, whether in one decade, as he has proposed, or in two or three decades. Or perhaps he understands the hurdles perfectly well but does not want to weaken the powerful message of the plan's benefits by acknowledging its looming challenges.

One of the biggest problems is his assumption that natural gas, which now generates about 22 percent of U.S. electricity, can be handily replaced by wind power. In America today, baseline power production is met by coal-fired stations and nuclear plants, which, respectively, work 70 percent and 90 percent of the time delivering electricity into the grid. Natural-gas power plants operate, on average, only 21 percent of the time, meeting peak demand on hot summer days and cold winter nights.

Under Pickens' plan, wind turbines would produce the same amount of electricity—22 percent—as natural gas currently does. But wind is a fickle source of power, so to be available on demand—as natural gas now is—considerably more turbines would have to be constructed than envisioned in his plan. Only detailed simulations of generation and consumption patterns could determine the actual number of turbines, their optimal locations, and the requisite high-voltage (HV) interconnections needed to substitute one form of generation for another—and no such simulations have been done.

Pickens' projections about how many new turbines will be needed under his plan, as well as the rate of constructing new transmission lines, also are highly optimistic. In 2007, U.S. utilities installed about 3,200 turbines with a total generating capacity of 5.24 gigawatts of electricity: If these turbines were to generate electricity 25 percent of the time—a typical load factor—they would produce enough electricity for about one million households for a year. (The U.S. has more than 110 million households.) But even if today's natural gas-fired power plant capacity were replaced at an unrealistic 1:1 ratio by wind turbines, Pickens is talking about installing 40 gigawatts of wind power a year—roughly 8 times the 2007 pace. And even if the turbines were to average 3 megawatts (larger than today's mean), some 130,000 of them would be needed. With determination and ample financing, that is a plausible pace.

But the Pickens Plan also estimates spending $200 billion for building new high-voltage (HV) transmission links to carry electricity from the Great Plains to the coasts. Recent construction costs of HV lines have ranged from less than $2 million per mile to more than $5 million per mile; the latter rate would get America about 40,000 miles of new HV connections. Without knowing the specifics, which Pickens' plan do not address, this may or may not be enough to link nearly 400 gigawatts of newly installed wind-generating capacity in the Dakotas, Nebraska, Kansas, Oklahoma, and Texas with high urban concentrations on the coasts. In any case, the construction pace would be a huge challenge. During the 1990s, U.S. utilities built about 9,700 miles of new HV lines and plans for this decade amount to less than 8,000 miles—one-fifth to one-sixth of the 40,000 to 50,000 miles required under the Pickens plan.

The Limits of Pickens' Plan

And then there is the switch to natural gas vehicles. While they are efficient, clean, and entirely desirable (I had advocated their use as far back as the first oil "crisis" of 1973), scaling of their ownership to tens of millions units, from fewer than 200,000 such cars today, would be extremely difficult to do in a single decade—and only a few of America's nearly 120,000 service stations now offer natural gas. Unfortunately, America also is increasingly an importer of natural gas (buying 18 percent of total global consumption in 2007). And natural gas prices follow those of crude oil, a reality that could reduce the plan's eventual impact on the trade deficit—and sharply reducing this wealth transfer is one of Pickens' major goals.

The Texas oilman [Pickens] is right: This is a crisis of America's own making.

Finally, a sobering thought about the efficacy of the Pickens Plan to prevent the massive wealth transfer that the Texan rightly abhors. If oil prices were to stabilize at the level prevailing in mid-August 2008, then Middle Eastern exporters will end up earning nearly one trillion dollars for their heavy, sulfurous crudes in 2008. Unchanged or growing oil imports, with prices staying well above $100 per barrel, would translate to an outflow of some $10 trillion in a decade. But even if the Pickens plan were to reduce that by more than a third, the country would still be running a huge trade deficit that precludes the re-emergence of a strong dollar: Given America's large budget deficit and more than $40 trillion of assorted debts and uncovered obligations, even a perfect realization of the Pickens Plan would still leave the U.S. on a weakening economic trajectory.

The Texas oilman is right: This is a crisis of America's own making. Federal mileage standards doubled America's passenger car fuel efficiency between 1976 and 1986, to 27.5 mpg. But with the ensuing decades of inexpensive oil, no new standards were set. A mere continuation of the 1976–1986 rate of improvement would have meant that American cars today would average close to 50 mpg, eliminating the need for nearly 70 percent of the crude oil we import. Moreover, a massive adoption of SUVs pushed the passenger vehicle fleet performance to just 22 mpg by 2006. And if America hopes to make up for its gasoline profligacy with more drilling, that will not prove to be effective solution: More oil will be discovered in America's offshore waters, but not nearly enough to make the country self-sufficient, even after two to three decades of such activity.

Unfortunately, nothing—and certainly not the Pickens Plan—offers an effective technical fix in just a decade. America's per capita energy consumption remains twice as high as the European Union's and Japan's. The era of Americans driving two SUVs to 5,000-square-foot houses 50 miles from city centers may be over. But for the U.S., even more radical, protracted and very painful adjustments will be needed to cure the nation's most incapacitating addiction.

Organizations to Contact

The editors have compiled the following list of organizations concerned with the issues debated in this book. The descriptions are derived from materials provided by the organizations. All have publications or information available for interested readers. The list was compiled on the date of publication of the present volume; the information provided here may change. Be aware that many organizations take several weeks or longer to respond to inquiries, so allow as much time as possible.

American Council for an Energy-Efficient Economy
529 14th Street NW, Suite 600, Washington, D.C. 20045
(202) 507-4000 • fax: (202) 429-2248
website: www.aceee.org

ACEEE actively participates in the energy debate, developing policy recommendations and documenting how energy efficiency measures can reduce energy use, air pollutant emissions, and greenhouse gas emissions while benefiting the economy. Founded in 1980 as a nonprofit organization, ACEEE publishes research reports including *Energy Efficiency in a Clean Energy Standard*.

American Petroleum Institute (API)
1220 L Street NW, Washington, DC 20005
(202) 682-8000
website: www.api.org

The American Petroleum Institute (API) is a national trade organization that represents approximately 400 oil producers, refiners, suppliers, pipeline operators, marine transporters, and service and supply companies. In recent years, API has grown internationally to advocate for policies that support the oil industry worldwide. It also offers research on industry trends, sponsors research ranging from economic analyses to toxicology, disseminates environmental health and safety regulations and information, and reports on recent drilling activities and technological progress. The API provides certification programs for oil industry professionals, as well as safety, environmental health, and quality control training. API publishes numerous books, pamphlets, training and safety manuals, statistical research, and newsletters each year.

Association for the Study of Peak Oil and Gas (ASPO)

Klintvagen 42, SE-756 55 Uppsala
  Sweden
+46 471 76 43
e-mail: mikaelhook@fysast.uu.se
website: www.peakoil.net

The Association for the Study of Peak Oil and Gas (ASPO) is a network of scientists focusing on the study of peak oil and the economic and scientific consequences of the oil production decline. ASPO strives to determine an accurate date for the point of peak oil and spread awareness of the consequences of less oil on oil-dependent countries. The ASPO newsletter is published monthly, and some regions are producing their own newsletters. Because of its scholarly work in the field, ASPO also offers statistical information on the subject, as well as a number of academic theses, peer-reviewed articles, and books providing valuable insight into the topic of peak oil. All of these resources can be found on the ASPO website.

The Brookings Institution

1775 Massachusetts Ave. NW, Washington, DC 20036
(202) 797-6000 • fax: (202) 797-6004
e-mail: Communications@brookings.edu
website: www.brookings.edu

The Brookings Institution is a private nonprofit organization devoted to conducting independent research and developing solutions to complex domestic and international problems. The organization's goal is to provide high-quality analysis and recommendations for decision-makers on the full range of challenges facing an increasingly interdependent world. The Brooking Institution Press publishes multiple titles including, *The Arab Awakening* in 2011.

Independent Petroleum Association of America (IPAA)

1201 15th St. NW, Suite 300, Washington, DC 20005
(202) 857-4722 • fax: (202) 857-4799
website: www.ipaa.org

The Independent Petroleum Association of America (IPAA) is a national trade association representing independent oil and natural gas producers and service companies, who develop 90 percent of domestic oil and gas wells, produce 68 percent of domestic oil and produce 82 percent of domestic natural gas. IPAA advocates and lobbies for the interests of its members with the U.S. Congress, federal agencies, and the executive administration. It also researches and provides economic and statistical information about the exploration and development of offshore wells. The IPAA publishes a weekly newsletter, *Washington Report*, which covers legislative and regulatory issues in the industry. The IPAA website also provides a broad range of reports and statistical studies covering the oil and gas industry and supply-and-demand forecasts.

Institute for Energy Research (IER)

1100 H St. NW, Suite 400, Washington, DC 20005
(202) 621-2950 • fax: (202) 637-2420
website: www.instituteforenergyresearch.org

Founded in 1989, The Institute for Energy Research (IER) is a not-for-profit organization that conducts intensive research and analysis on the functions, operations, and government regulation of global energy markets. IER promotes the idea that unfettered energy markets provide the most efficient and effective solutions to today's global energy and environmental challenges and works to educate legislators, policymakers, and the public to the vital role offshore drilling plays in our energy future. It publishes various fact sheets and comprehensive studies on renewable and nonrenewable energy sources, the growing green economy, climate change, and offshore oil exploration and drilling opportunities. IER also maintains a blog on its website, which provides timely comment on relevant energy and legislative issues.

National Commission on Energy Policy

1225 I Street NW, Suite 1000, Washington, D.C. 20005
(202) 204-2400 • fax: (202) 637-9220
e-mail: info@energycommission.org
website: www.energycommission.org

The National Commission on Energy Policy is a bipartisan organization that conducts research on the rapidly changing landscape of energy needs, vulnerabilities and opportunities, with the aim of strengthening the economy, safeguarding national security and protecting the global environment and public health. The National Commission on Energy Policy publishes a number of reports, including *Task Force on America's Future Energy Jobs* in 2011.

Union of Concerned Scientists (UCS)

Two Brattle Square, Cambridge, MA   02138
(617) 547-5552 • fax: (617) 864-9405
website: www.ucsusa.org

Founded by scientists and students at MIT in 1969, the Union of Concerned Scientists (UCS) is the leading science-based nonprofit working for a healthy environment and a safer world. UCS utilizes independent scientific research and citizen action "to develop innovative, practical solutions and to secure responsible changes in government policy, corporate practices, and consumer choices." UCS publishes in-depth reports on several important issues: global warming, scientific integrity, clean energy and vehicles, global security, and food and agriculture. It also publishes the *Catalyst* magazine, *Earthwise* newsletter, and *Greentips Newsletter*.

US Energy Association (USEA)

1300 Pennsylvania Ave. NW, Suite 550, Mailbox 142
Washington, DC   20004
(202) 312-1230 • fax: (202) 682-1682
e-mail: jhammond@usea.org
website: www.usea.org

The United States Energy Association (USEA) is an association of public and private energy-related organizations, corporations, and government agencies that promotes the varied interests of the US energy sector by disseminating information about energy issues. In conjunction with the US Agency for International Development and the US Department of Energy, USEA sponsors the Energy Partnership Program as well as numerous policy reports and conferences dealing with global and domestic energy issues. USEA also organizes trade and educational exchange visits with other countries. It also provides information on presidential initiatives, governmental agencies, and national service organizations.

Bibliography

Books

Andrew Scott Cooper	*The Oil Kings: How the U.S., Iran, and Saudi Arabia Change the Balance of Power in the Middle East.* New York: Simon & Schuster, 2011.
Daniel Dicker	*Oil's Endless Bid: Taming the Unreliable Price of Oil to Secure Our Economy.* Hoboken, NJ: Wiley, 2011.
Morgan Downey	*Oil 101.* New York: Wooden Table, 2009.
John S. Duffield	*Over a Barrel: The Costs of U.S. Foreign Oil Dependence.* Stanford, CA: Stanford University, 2008.
Thad Dunning	*Crude Democracy: Natural Resource Wealth and Political Regimes.* New York: Cambridge, 2008.
Leah McGrath Goodman	*The Asylum: The Renegades Who Hijacked the World's Oil Market.* New York: William Morrow, 2011.
Jay E. Hakes	*A Declaration of Energy Independence: How Freedom from Foreign Oil Can Improve National Security, Our Economy, and the Environment.* Hoboken, NJ: Wiley, 2008.
Kent Moors	*The Vega Factor: Oil Volatility and the Next Global Crisis.* Hoboken, NJ: Wiley, 2011.

Lewis Reynolds   *America the Prisoner: The*
                        Implications of Foreign Oil Addiction
                        and a Realistic Plan to End It.
                        Charlotte, NC: Relevance Media,
                        2010.

Michael L. Ross   *The Oil Curse: How Petroleum Wealth*
                        Shapes the Development of Nations.
                        Princeton, NJ: Princeton University
                        Press, 2012.

Vaclav Smil   *Oil: A Beginner's Guide.* Oxford,
                        England: Oneworld, 2008.

Daniel Yergin   *The Prize: The Epic Quest for Oil,*
                        Money, & Power. New York: Simon &
                        Schuster, 1991.

Daniel Yergin   *The Quest: Energy, Security, and the*
                        Remaking of the Modern World. New
                        York: Penguin, 2011.

Periodicals and Internet Sources

Advanced Energy   "Americans See High Energy Costs
Economy   Ahead but Bullish That Advanced
                        Energy Can Solve Problems,
                        Strengthen Economy," December 15,
                        2011. www.aee.net.

Automotive News   "Ethanol Isn't the Answer; Picking
                        Winners Never Is," January 9, 2012.

Hembree   "Alternative Energy: Ending
Brandon   Dependence on Mideast Oil," *Western*
                        Farm Press, July 18, 2011.

E   "The Big Spill," July–August 2010.

The Economist   "Repairing America's Roads: It Tolls for Thee," May 20, 2010.

The Economist   "Barack Obama's Energy Policy: Recycled," March 31, 2011.

Sandra I. Erwin   "Air Force: To Save Fuel, We Must Change How We Fly," *National Defense*, July 2010.

Michael G. Frodl and John M. Manoyan   "Untapped Resource: Natural Gas, Safer Cleaner Energy That Pays for Itself," *National Defense*, May 2009.

Marc Goldman   "Breaking Our Oil Addiction," *inFocus*, Fall 2009.

Lee Harnack   "Ending Our Oil Dependence," *Mass Transit*, November 23, 2010.

Tom Hayward   "Gulf Storms Flattening Dream of Reducing Need for Foreign Crude," *Natural Gas Week*, September 15, 2008.

William P. Hoar   "Promoting Pain at the Pump," *New American*, May 24, 2011.

Paul Livingston   "The Future of Fossil Fuel?" *R & D*, June 9, 2011.

Ron MacKinnon   "Accepting Renewable Energy," *Construction Today*, March 2011.

Margaret Menge and Ashley Martella   "Robbie Diamond: US Must Shed Oil Dependence," *Newsmax*, November 22, 2011.

Paul Roberts "The Last Drops," *Popular Science*, July 2011.

Hillary Rosner "The Low-Hanging Fruit," *Popular Science*, July 2011.

Tom Steyer and "We Don't Need More Foreign Oil
John Podesta and Gas," *Wall Street Journal*, January 24, 2012.

Hugh Tomlinson "Coping with Falling Volumes," *Middle East Economic Digest*, November 13, 2009.

USA Today "Housing Crisis Linked to Foreign Oil Dependency," November 2010.

Index

E

F